An Ecumenical Pilgrimage

Other books by Paul Rowntree Clifford

Now is the Time, Collins, London, 1970
Interpreting Human Experience, Collins, London, 1971
The Death of the Dinosaur, SPCK, London, 1978
Politics and the Christian Vision, SCM Press, London, 1984
Government by the People?, SCM Press, London, 1986

In publication:

The Kingdom of God: Fact or Fiction?, Eerdmans, Grand Rapids, Michigan, Spring 1995

AN ECUMENICAL PILGRIMAGE

Paul Rowntree Clifford

West Ham Central Mission
London
1994

Published 1994 by the West Ham Central Mission
409 Barking Road, Plaistow, London, E13 8AL

© *1994 by Paul Rowntree Clifford and the West Ham Central Mission*

ISBN 0 9524521 0 3

Cover design by Cartwright Designs, Little Walden, Essex, CB10 1XA

Typeset and produced for the publisher by Yard Publishing Services, Shudy Camps, Cambs, CB1 6RE

Printed by Antony Rowe Ltd, Bumpers's Farm, Chippenham, SN14 6QA

British Cataloguing-in-Publication Data. A catalogue record for this book is obtainable from the British Library

CONTENTS

FOREWORD

by DR PHILIP MORGAN,
Formerly General Secretary to the British Council of Churches

I AM GLAD TO commend this autobiography covering a period of sixty years of remarkable social change and ecumenical development. To tell the tale of a life spanning the years 1913 to 1993 inevitably promises a fascinating picture of changing worlds hardly credible to a modern generation. Add to that both personal involvement at the centre of things and a capacity for reflection and analysis, and we get what this autobiography is – a series of insights into one man's ecumenical pilgrimage which illuminates a sucession of historical periods and their significance for us and the future.

For me four periods stand out. The first, the years before and during the Second World War when Paul Rowntree Clifford, first through his parents, and then in his own right, was involved in that extraordinary phenomenon, the West Ham Central Mission. Its work was so comprehensive, its circle of support so wide and eminent and its latent ecumenism so in advance of its time.

Canada and McMaster University provide the setting for a different pioneering role, at the same time enabling the author to identify the onset of that economic, business model which sets aside all other standards save satisfactory accountancy to the detriment of much that is human.

He came to Selly Oak where the issue was missiology, engagement with a changing world in the name of the gospel. The ecumenical contribution here was to enlarge from British to European, from single discipline to multi-discipline, and from one faith to dialogue with all other faiths.

This is a pilgrimage ecumenical in the fullest sense, not only engaged with divisions of the Church, but also seeking unity of all things in Christ. It is an ecumenical pilgrimage, for the journey is of faith with the end not yet in sight.

Chapter One

FAMILY BACKGROUND

MY FIRST REACTION to the suggestion that I should write my autobiography was that it would be pretentious to do so. Biographies are mainly written by or about those who are in the public eye or have played a prominent part in public life, the account of whose experiences is of general interest and an important contribution to the historical record of their time. The life of anyone who has not been famous, however varied and unusual his or her experience may have been, will not generally command the attention of a publisher or be thought to be of anything but passing interest to a few people. Nevertheless, we are curious about what has happened to others, especially if they are those with whom we can identify and yet whose experience has been somewhat different from our own. When pressed by one of my friends and former colleagues to recapture memories of events and people he had known, I decided to write my memoirs for my family circle and those like himself who might be interested, encouraged at the same time to believe that they may also have wider interest.

I have never kept a diary and I am one of those people who is ruthless about getting rid of papers. It has always been my practice to tear up the minutes of meetings in which I have participated on the assumption that I could always refer to the official record of the secretary if I wished to do so. This kept filing to a minimum and proved to be a boon when I retired and no longer enjoyed the benefit of secretaries and an office. I am, therefore, mainly dependent on memory which is highly selective and sometimes inaccurate. But in writing about one's past it does act as a built-in editor and helps to separate the significant from the insignificant.

We take memory for granted, but it is a most mysterious faculty which the invention of computers has done little to illuminate. What they can store and recover depends entirely on what human beings feed into them; the activity of reaching back into the past and selecting what is brought back to the mind in vivid imagery defies explanation. We only know that we do it, but how we do so is beyond our comprehension. The eminent philosopher, Bertrand Russell, once toyed with the idea that remembering was direct acquaintance with past events similar to acquaintance with objects presented to the senses, while others, finding this equation unacceptable, have found themselves doubting the correspondence of images of memory to that to which they purport to refer. But such scepticism, if seriously adopted, would make no sense of our common experience and would undermine the foundation for all practical activity. We depend on the validity of memory for all conscious and purposive action even though we may not understand how it works.

Biographies that go beyond the reach of memory and depend on written records for tracing the lineage and forbears of the subject can become very complicated and even boring for the reader. But family history is a necessary background for understanding how anybody has come to be the person that he or she is. I can largely restrict myself to those whom I remember, for my grandparents on both my father's and mother's sides are shadowy figures of whom little of importance comes to mind. As a very small boy I remember my father's mother as an ancient matriarchal figure in a black dress with an indomitable will who obviously had held all the family together and impressed her personality on them all. Her husband, who died before I was born, was a skilled Sunderland shipwright, but clearly the junior partner in the marriage; my father rarely spoke of him; it was his mother who was the formative influence on his early years. Her own mother's first marriage had been to the vicar of Yarm in Yorkshire, presumably a family living, but one which raised difficulties for his conscience since he could not reconcile doubts about infant baptism with the tenets of the Church of England. Consequently he resigned his incumbency, but on his death my great grandmother had all six children christened around his coffin! That may well have contributed to the strength of purpose inherited by my father through his own mother.

I do not remember my maternal grandmother, though I was told she was a gentle, loving person to whom my mother was deeply attached. Her husband was a small landowner who like his cousins owned farms in Leicestershire, one of which was named after the hawthorn bush on which Richard III hung his crown at the battle of Bosworth. The family traced its origins back through lands in North Wales to a distant ancestor, one of the first garter knights to hang his banner in St George's Windsor in the fourteenth century. My grandfather was unusually gifted. At the early age of eleven he invented the chain which was copied and later patented for use on bicycles, though he derived no financial reward for doing so. He was a man of considerable independence of mind; he would not allow the use of barbed wire on his farms and refused to give access to the hunt. Later he became concerned with the manufacture of fertilisers and their use on the land. I simply remember seeing him on one occasion as an old man with a white beard who was cared for by his youngest daughter, Dot, in a terraced house in Coundon Road, Coventry. This is as far back as my hazy recollections go, and I leave the pursuit of the Clifford genealogy to my cousin, David, who is an enthusiastic researcher into family history and is number 1 in the membership list of the Clifford society which now has widespread ramifications in this country and overseas.

My father was born in 1867, the eldest son in what today would be considered a large family. He was named Robert Rowntree – the latter being the maiden name of his grandmother and subsequently passed on to my brother and myself and later to our children. My father had three younger sisters and four brothers – two children having died in infancy. I never knew Fred, the eldest of these brothers; he died at an early age leaving one daughter, Etta, who came to live with my grandmother and whom I looked upon more as an aunt than a cousin. The third of the brothers was Alfred who became a highly successful and prosperous estate agent. He had five children, the fourth of whom, Derek, became well known as an authority on the Norwich school of artists and an expert on gardens and horticulture, about which he has written a number of books, notably about the culture of geraniums. His son, Timothy, is a leading figure in the art world, having been director of the Manchester gallery and now of the National Galleries of Scotland.

The fourth of the brothers was Ernest, the father of David mentioned above. He was an enthusiastic footballer and nearly signed professional forms for Sunderland. However, he went to Oxford at the instigation of my father to prepare for the Baptist ministry and secured admission to St Catherine's, then the society for non-collegiate students. My uncle always thought that some snobbery was attached to this and that was the reason why he narrowly missed his 'blue'. After Oxford, on completing his training at Regent's Park College in London, Ernest became an army chaplain in the First World War and on demobilisation joined my father as a colleague in the ministry at West Ham, of which more later.

The youngest brother, Elden, was a bachelor and the London managing director of the wire-rope manufacturers, Glaholm and Robson. He lived in a club in Bloomsbury until his retirement when he joined his sisters in what had become the family home in Woburn Sands. The eldest of these, Mary, left the old home in Sunderland to keep house for my father when he settled in the ministry at West Ham and remained there for the whole of her life until retirement. The other two sisters, Aura and Phia, were schoolteachers and stayed in Sunderland. Aura became a highly respected headmistress and was the anchor of the family home in Beechwood Terrace where, with my cousin Etta, she cared for my grandmother until her death soon after the end of the Second World War. Beechwood Terrace was home to all the members of the family who gravitated to it for holidays and visits. My earliest memories are of being taken there in the summer, of tram rides to Roker with bucket and spade to play on the sands, of walks in the parks and coming home to number 7 for the warmth of a family welcome and the 'Sunderland cake' and ginger nuts which were a special feature of every visit. My father always talked of visits to Sunderland as 'going home' and, although I have lived in many different places, I have always felt that my roots were there. Such is the influence of the very early years. Phia married a merchant sea captain, but they made their home with Aura and Etta, being joined after the Second World War by Mary and Elden on their retirement. They then needed a larger house than the two adjoining ones at the top of Beechwood Terrace which Aura and Phia had built to accommodate the extended family. Ernest had also retired to a cottage in Woburn Sands, and so with Elden's help the rest acquired a large property there where they lived for several years until the deaths of Aura and Phia's husband Len. Mary, Elden, Phia and Etta then moved to a house in Sutton where they all ended their days. This pleasant suburban villa was the last family home, but whenever I went there in these latter years I always felt that I was going back to Sunderland.

I have no such memories of my mother's background. Her brothers and sisters were individualists and somewhat eccentric; the Bannister family seemed to have little in common and a faint aura of mystery hung over the home from which they came. My mother rarely spoke of her elder brother, Will, and then with embarrassment. Apparently he was intellectually brilliant but became addicted to gambling and through that brought considerable damage to the family fortunes. I never saw him and I believe my mother had lost all contact with him before I was born. Her younger brother, Steve, was something of an enigma. He played the role of a social misfit and, unlike his sisters, prided himself on belonging to a working class culture which in fact was not the case. Dorothy, always referred to as Dot, looked after her father, as I have said, until his death. She was a complicated character – a gifted musician, but deprived of opportunity and in many ways out of tune with the world in which she found herself living. Bombed out of Coventry during the Nazi raids on that city, she ended her days shortly after the war in Frinton-on-Sea in a house which my mother had acquired for her.

Her other sister, Amy, was a strange and to a child a somewhat frightening character. She was the star sister of her generation at St Bartholemew's hospital and went as a volunteer nurse with the British army to the Middle East during the First World War. After the armistice she married Hugh Walsham, a leading authority on diseases of the chest and one of the pioneers in radiology. He was a consultant at Bart's and that was where they met. They lived in his large four-storey house in Harley Street, and as small boys my brother and I were sent to stay with them from time to time, partly, I think, as a form of appeasement for the fact that my mother had chosen to live and work in the East End of London; for my aunt behaved as if she was a member of the aristocracy, acting the part of the Lady Bountiful and using the royal 'We' when referring to the social status she had assumed. These visits were somewhat overwhelming to small boys, though I remember with admiration the kindness of uncle Peter, as we called him, who allowed me to watch him in his consulting room as he experimented with the fascinating, sparklimg, though unprotected equipment which he used in those early days of radiography. He wore white gloves on both hands as a form of protection, but when I knew him he had lost most of his fingers and died in the mid nineteen-twenties as a result of his pioneering work.

My aunt then spent a considerable time first in Vienna and afterwards in Florence before returning to her beloved London where she lived in a succession of flats until the end of the Second World War when she moved to rooms in Coventry, eking out the small capital her husband had left her. She was by then nearly blind, but continued fiercely independent, having lost all her friends and acquaintances, and died practically penniless in a nursing home at the great age of 92.

My mother was the only member of the family to find real fulfilment. She left home in her late teens to work at a centre for deprived children at Northfield in Birmingham. As a girl within her complicated family set-up she had found an anchorage in the life of Salem, Longford, the Baptist chapel near her home, and her life-long friend was the daughter of the minister. She looked to Salem rather than her home as the rock from which she was hewn and to the end of her life cherished her connection with it. It was against this background that she decided to train as a Baptist deaconess in London, working mainly in the Italian community, and it was from there she went to West Ham in circumstances to which I shall refer later and remained there for the rest of her life.

These two very different family backgrounds came together in the marriage of my father and mother in 1910 and three years later I was born into a home and missionary environment in which I was to spend the first half of my life. But before embarking on my own reminiscences I have to go back to my father's early years, the road which led him to East London and the establishment of the West Ham Central Mission and the remarkable life-long partnership which he and my mother shared.

My father left school at fourteen years of age with the desire to be apprenticed in the drawing office of the Sunderland shipyards, but his father was a quiet unassuming man who was either unwilling or unable to make the necessary arrangements. Consequently he found himself apprenticed to a blacksmith in the yards, a skilled and difficult craft of which he himself became a master. In his spare time he began to see a good deal of his relatives the Rowntrees. They were Baptists and members of the Lindsay Road church with which they persuaded him to become associated. There he met his life-long friend, Walter Speed, the son of the minister. Speed was three years older than my father and exercised a profound influence upon him, constantly challenging his ambition and spurring him to new efforts. After my father had been baptized and joined the church, Speed began to encourage him to think of the ministry, but the obstacles were formidable as he lacked the necessary educational qualifications. London university matriculation was the hurdle and my father joined his friend in evening classes to secure the requirement for entry into a theological college.

The story of these years of preparation is an epic of determination. My father began work in the shipyard at six o'clock in the morning, knocking off at five. He came home tired and dirty after a day's work, changed his clothes and, after a meal, began the evening's study; he worked until he could keep awake no longer. But the evenings were not enough. Out of his meagre earnings he paid another man to do his job on Saturday mornings so that he could give the whole of the day to study. Opportunities for sport and normal recreation were denied him by his own choice, but he achieved his object and was admitted to Regent's Park College, then in London, for ministerial training.

In those days the theological degree for which the men of Regent's Park entered was the Senatus Academicus of the Associated Theological Colleges. The stiff curriculum meant a hard slog for him, working alongside men who were on the whole far more educationally advanced. He took the examination at the end of his fifth year and was placed in the first division of the class list:

a fine achievement in the light of his early struggles. At the end of his course he was invited to become minister of the Barking Road Tabernacle in the heart of London's dockland. This little church had fallen on hard times; it had been riven with contention; the previous minister had left in disgrace; there was a debt on the building, and the small deputation that waited on the Principal of Regent's Park looking for a young man who would tackle such a daunting prospect could hardly have expected to be led out of their difficulties by someone with such indomitable determination.

My father set himself to restore the self-respect and confidence of the congregation. He became convinced that the way to do this was to clear the debt on the building and he resolved to make this the test of whether he was meant to stay as their minister. At the beginning of 1899 the debt stood at £881, a large sum for a small congregation in those days. When it had been reduced by only £21 by the end of March my father challenged them to raise the whole sum by the time of the second anniversary of his induction in the following November. The people responded magnificently, giving all that they could and persuading their friends to help. By the end of October they had raised over £600 and they were overjoyed that the millstone which had so long hung around their necks was at last in sight of being lifted.

Not so my father; he was bitterly disappointed; the target had not been reached and he felt he had to resign following his anniversary meeting which was shortly to take place. Then occurred one of those unpredictable events which was to change the course of the lives of very many people and without which this autobiography would never have been written. Just before the date fixed for the meeting my father received a letter from a complete stranger in Chelmsford signed by a certain Isaac Saunders inquiring whether the debt on the chapel had been wiped out. My father replied telling him what had happened and explaining that the church was now exhausted and could do no more. He received another letter from this unknown correspondent promising a gift of £15 if the people would make one more effort. £15 was a good deal of money in those days and my father thought that anybody who could promise such a sum must be a wealthy man who could probably afford to be even more generous; and so he felt that he must go to Chelmsford and see this potential benefactor.

When he arrived at the station he asked to be directed to the address he had been given, a house called Broomfield. He was told that this must be the name of a village some two miles away and so he set out to walk there in the hope of finding the man who had written to him. On asking for directions to the house of Mr Saunders, he was told that the only person of that name was an old man living in a cottage down the village street. Although he thought this could not be the benefactor for whom he was looking, he had come a long way and his curiosity had been aroused. Knocking at the cottage door, it was opened by an old man well over eighty years of age, wearing a leather apron. His hands were gnarled with manual toil and it was evident that he was at work.

My father introduced himself by name and said he was looking for a Mr Isaac Saunders. Could the old man help him?

'Come in sir' was the reply. 'I wrote to you yesterday and I am very glad to see you; come in and sit down'.

My father entered a small two-roomed cottage, the ground floor of which was sparsely furnished with a wooden bench on which the old man's tailoring work was spread; the rest of the space was occupied by one or two primitive articles. The only place to sit down appeared to be a seat at the end of a fender which guarded the fireplace. As my father looked round the cottage with its evident signs of poverty, he felt himself compelled to ask how the old man could have afforded to promise to send him £15.

'If you will get up from where you are sitting', the old man said, 'and hand me the little black book under the cushion where I keep my accounts, I will show you. You see, sir, I earn thirty pounds a year. Out of this I set aside six pounds for the Lord's work, and the last entry, as you will see, was made three years ago when I sent six pounds to the British and Foreign Bible Society to provide bibles for the Chinese. Every night and every morning I kneel down by that old fender on which you are sitting and pray that the Lord will bless and use the gift. But I haven't given anything for three years and so there is eighteen pounds laid up on the altar. Since writing to you the Lord has told me to give you the three pounds for this year. Take these', he said, passing over three golden sovereigns, 'and the other fifteen will follow.'

My father scarcely knew what to say. 'I can hardly accept this. You can't afford to give so much. You need someone to look after you.'

'Ah sir', said the old man with a twinkle in his eye, 'females are expensive!'

My father loved to tell this part of the story; the old man's sense of humour appealed to him. Then my father asked him how he knew about the debt on the chapel.

'I knew nothing about you except what I read in something that was sent to me last year about the effort to clear off the debt on your chapel; but I talk a lot to the Lord. Take this and God bless your work.'

My father told me that he walked on air from the cottage to the station at Chelmsford; he was so overwhelmed by what had happened. In the compartment of the train he found himself sitting opposite a sea captain who had just left his ship at Tilbury, and he simply had to tell him about the old man. After hearing the story, his travelling companion offered to give him five pounds if he would promise to continue the work he had begun. He boarded the tram to take him back home, and opposite him was one of the members of the congregation who had already given generously. She promised another ten pounds. At the anniversary meeting my father told the story once more and the chairman said, 'We are going to clear the debt tonight'.

My father was acutely embarrassed. He had already made his final appeal to his people and had promised that he would not ask them for anything more. However, the chairman reminded my father that he was not presiding; it was *his* intention to make the appeal. Offering to give ten per cent of whatever was promised he persuaded the small company present to pledge sixty-six pounds, including a gift of ten pounds from a schoolteacher who had saved it to buy a bicycle. Hearing of this, another friend came forward with a promise of another fifty pounds and they were half-way to clearing the remaining debt. Then the fifteen sovereigns arrived by post from Isaac Saunders, each sewn up in a piece of silk. My father could not doubt any longer that his faith had been rewarded. A special church meeting was called at which it was decided to wipe off the debt completely by November 30th. When the day came not only had the target been reached, but there was a balance in hand of seventy-six pounds.

My father wrote to Isaac Saunders to tell him what had happened, sending him a copy of the magazine in which the whole story was told. The reply from the old man, which subsequently came into my possession, deserves quotation in full; for it enshrines the simple piety of one who never dreamt what the outcome of his gift would be.

Dear Sir,

I thank you for sending me the account of your gatherings in your December number. I was, and still am, exceedingly thankful that God has honoured me as an instrument by which the idea of a starting point was obtained. I do thank God most sincerely for all those whose hearts he did incline to take such an interest in this final movement and I rejoice with them all that God has crowned their efforts with abundant success. In the first letter I received from you, you said 'The schoolrooms are in a bad condition and we almost feel compelled to do something in the matter'. You say now 'Things must be quiet for some time'. You and your men of business know this is, and will be, an expensive time when men want 10p an hour. If God should spare our lives I shall be glad to see you to know about how you are getting on, but not until the Spring gets up and the buttercups and daisies are in bloom; then I can take you into a meadow where I walk, think and pray. At present I cannot promise to assist you in your future movements, as in March last I promised to adopt a Christian young girl in India and paid ten pounds for her last two year's maintenance. At present I do not know how much my teacher of truth is to cost me.

I remain,
Yours respectfully.

Isaac Saunders

With the receipt of this letter and the clearance of the debt my father had the impetus to embark on building up the church over the next six years. But new challenges had to be faced. By the turn of the century West Ham was beginning to be the scene of widespread and extreme poverty which was soon to shock the conscience of the nation. In 1902 seven thousand men were out of work in the docks and starvation faced many homes. No unemployment benefit was available and my father was in the forefront of the battle to bring assistance to those in dire need. He was appointed secretary of the relief fund in his own ward and worked unceasingly at all hours of the day and night to do whatever he could to alleviate the distress. The sight of human suffering moved him to the depths of his being, and he never spared himself. Allied with this compassion for his fellow men was a burning hatred of injustice; it was the only hatred of his life.

Conditions got worse. The winter of 1904/5 was a terrible one and starvation was a reality in many homes. No longer could my father and his people battle alone without help from outside and by then the plight of people in the East End of London had begun to feature in the national press. My father, therefore, opened his manse to any who would come and help in the emergency and two deaconesses from their headquarters in Guildford Street were invited to form the spearhead of a large staff of full-time members and voluntary workers, leading to the establishment of the West Ham Central Mission as an institutional church with a widespread social outreach. My mother was one of these two deaconesses and, with her imagination, vision and drive, became the dominant partner in the whole enterprise.

Soon after her arrival she organized a visitation of the district with a view to starting a service for women on Monday afternoons, since Sunday was a day when most of them could not get to church with all they had to do in their homes. They had to bear the brunt of all the poverty caused by the unemployment of their husbands and my mother knew that they stood in the greatest need of help. On the first Monday afternoon 500 filled the church for the first service and the number rapidly grew to over 1000. Between the wars the number had to be restricted to 2500, and to keep their places they had to join again every year. This was but one of the ventures undertaken to meet the needs of the neighbourhood, though it was undoubtedly the most far-reaching one, influencing virtually every street in the district.

The full story of these years leading up to the First World War is told in a book I wrote in 1950 entitled *Venture In Faith*. Suffice it to say here that the arrival of my mother in 1905 and the founding of the West Ham Central Mission is the background which explains all that subsequently happened to me.

In 1910, after my father's visit to the United States to explore what was being done there to combat the problem of poverty, they were married from my mother's old home to the delight of all their friends and colleagues. The service was conducted by Dr John Clifford, the leading Nonconformist minister and social reformer of the pre-war years. He was no blood relative, but my father greatly admired him and looked to him as a model for his own ministry. Three years after the wedding I was born not only into their home but into the life of the Mission they had founded.

Chapter Two

SCHOOL DAYS

B Y THE TIME I was born on 21 February 1913 Holly House, the former manse, had already become the residence for the growing staff. Plans were already at an advanced stage for clearing the site and building a new church on it. This entailed the acquisition of fresh premises to provide a Settlement House for the expanding staff. But the outbreak of war necessitated the postponement of the plans, and the work of the Mission for the time being had to be concentrated in the old Tabernacle down the road and other makeshift accommodation. Holly House was in any case too small, and since it was to be demolished anyway to make room for the new church when circumstances permitted my father and mother acquired a row of old cottages and shops further up the road for conversion to what was to become the Marnham House Settlement, named after a prominent Baptist layman who was chairman of the building committee for the proposed new church.

Materials were in short supply due to the exigencies of war, but Holly House was carefully dismantled and everything that could be salvaged was pressed into use. Bricks, doors, windows, woodwork, all went into the patchwork and, under the eye of an architect who had considerable artistic gifts, the Hostel, as it was called, was completed and ready for occupation by 1916. With its latticed windows and stucco front, it provided a sharp contrast to the unimaginative buildings on the main road. As the visitor entered through a wide arched doorway, the hall, from which opened a spacious dining room, gave the impression of a Tudor residence. Slats of wood across the ceilings produced the illusion of an oak-beamed roof and the ugliness of the two disused shops and two broken-down cottages had been transformed into the beauty of a country home.

My father and mother occupied one wing with my aunt Mary. She presided over the rest of the establishment where the staff and visiting volunteers had separate rooms. All met together for meals in the large dining room. Thus my first home was in the midst of a community and my earliest memory is of sheltering in the cellar of one of the old cottages with the rest of the residents of Marnham House during one of the air raids. It would have given us scant protection if a bomb had fallen on the building, but in those days air raids were a novelty and their infrequency simply added to the alarm. My brother, Hugh, who was three and a half years younger than I, had just been born, and the presence of a baby in the cellar heightened the protectiveness of the whole community.

I remember nothing else of the war except the excitement of armistice day, looking out of an upstairs window at people waving flags. The only other memories of these early years are my disappointment at being told of the birth of my brother when I expected the present of a box of chocolates and the celebration of my fourth Christmas with the gift of a little toy milk cart with imitation churns which I could push around the nursery. My delight in this is associated with the memory of the Salvation Army band playing carols in front of the adjoining shops. Perhaps this has something to do with my love of bands and processions and the regard I have always had for the Salvation Army.

My mother's father was concerned for our education and provided the money to engage a governess for my brother and me, a certain Miss Gadd, who was a member of the Plymouth Brethren and who sought to instil in us a healthy fear of the Lord. She was not a great success, though I do remember learning by heart the declension of the Latin word for table. She had the greatest difficulty in persuading us to say our prayers, but my principal memory is that of hitting her over the head with the stick of a feather brush and I think that was probably the end of the poor woman's attempt to instil in us some form of discipline. At any rate my mother did not try to secure a replacement for her and for a short time I was sent to the kindergarten of the West Ham High School for girls at Stratford. By the time I was eight years of age my father and mother had been lent a house in South Woodford within easy walking distance of St Aubyn's Preparatory School, more generally known in the area as 'Crumps', so named after the two sisters who had owned and presided over it for many years. My brother's and my first term coincided with the transfer of ownership to Colonel Colley who, after a distinguished war record, had been a master at Uppingham. This brought the standards of the school up to scratch and it is doubtful whether anywhere else provided a better educational grounding for small boys.

The mistresses on the staff were excellent, Miss Price running the most junior form of five-year-olds with skill and imagination and Miss Wilson grounding the older boys in arithmetic and algebra. The assistant masters were competent above the average and standards were set by Colonel Colley's teaching of Latin and insistence that boys should be well prepared for the Common Entrance examination for public schools. The French master made a lasting impression on me and, I suspect, on many other boys. His name was Msr Gebel, a Frenchman who had a flair for making the subject exciting. He taught it like a game and I remember being lined up with the other boys in the form and questions being asked in French from the top end downwards. If the first boy did not know the answer or could not respond correctly the question was passed down the line until someone succeeded; he was then promoted above the first boy who was questioned. The competition and excitement were intense. To this day I can handle the language reasonably well and I owe my grounding in it to the way I was taught at St Aubyn's.

Nevertheless, there is one matter on which I look back with regret. I was set Charles Kingsley's *Westward Ho* and Scott's *Ivanhoe* as a summer holiday task, and I vividly remember my mother's persistent efforts to get me to read a few pages every morning when I wanted to go and play on the beach. I was not ready for it and my painful efforts to concentrate on what did not interest me induced the feeling that classical English literature was to be avoided if at all possible, with the result that when I was a little older I missed the enjoyment of reading Scott, Dickens and Thackeray and the other great English novelists, and had to come to them much later in life. More seriously, it sowed the seeds of the expectation that learning of any kind could not be an exciting exploration, but must of necessity be a hard grind. This was to dog me throughout my school-days and I only really broke free from it in the last year of my undergraduate course. Since then throughout a long academic career I have become convinced that much of the defect in our educational system is the failure to build on the natural curiosity of the small child and impose adult requirements which stultify the learning process.

But to return to my years at St Aubyn's. While we spent the weeks at the house in South Woodford, we were taken to the Settlement in West Ham for the weekends, where I think my parents must have retained their rooms at the end of the house; for I never felt that anywhere else was really home. These post-war years were the time of the remarkable expansion of the Mission and everything in our lives seemed to centre on a catalogue of exciting events. Immediately after the armistice Queen Mary had expressed the wish to visit the service for women on Monday afternoons and she came with only a couple of hours notice to stand on the platform before the crowded congregation in the old Tabernacle, all the members of which were dressed in black: evidence that practically every one of them had lost a husband or a relative in the carnage. The Queen was clearly deeply moved by the sight; for she had recently lost one of her own sons in action and my mother used to say she sensed a mutual wave of sympathy and rapport which was to be the precursor of many royal visits in the years ahead.

Plans also came to fruition for the building of a large Byzantine-style church on the site of Holly House which could seat upwards of 2000 people and which my parents dreamed could become the Free Church cathedral of the East End of London. The cost had risen to £68,000, far in excess of anything anticipated before the war. It was raised by gifts from churches all over the country and overseas as far as Australia and New Zealand. September 21st 1922 was the day fixed for the opening ceremony. The veteran Baptist leader, Dr John Clifford had promised to preach the sermon, but a few days beforehand his frail health failed him and the well-known preacher, Dr Charles Brown took his place, preaching from the text he had chosen. But Dr Clifford was able to be present and offered the dedicatory prayer. I was there and I remember being introduced to the grand old man. Tremendous crowds assembled, far more than could be accommodated in the church. They had come from all corners of the British Isles and represented the donors who had made possible the erection of the striking building with its two white domes.

On the following Monday afternoon 2000 women assembled outside the old Tabernacle and marched up the road behind the Salvation Army band to be received at the four main doors of the new church by four ladies who had made substantial contributions to the cost of the building. The district had never seen anything like it. My mother described it as 'Mother Coming Home'.

This was not all. One generous benefactor had provided the money for purchasing a house at Tiptree in Essex for a home for sick children who needed a spell away from the squalor of slum streets to regain their health. This was called Child Haven and

The Memorial Church, West Ham Central Mission, c. 1922

when larger premises were acquired in Shenfield, they were opened by the present Queen Mother, then Duchess of York, and she later became patron of the whole Mission. Another donor provided a club for men in the grounds surrounding the church and my uncle Ernest, on demobilization from the chaplaincy service in the army, joined my father to take charge of the men's work. He organized as many as eight football teams to compete in the various leagues round about and played in the first team himself. The membership of the church by now numbered over 1000 and, although the morning congregations were relatively small, the church was often crowded to capacity on Sunday evenings. The whole place was bustling with activity with organizations and clubs of all kinds for those of every age.

This was the atmosphere I absorbed at weekends and during the school holidays. It was, therefore, not surprising that it should be assumed that when I grew up I would be ordained and join my father as his assistant and ultimate successor. This was the destiny mapped out for me from these early years. That my path should diverge in other directions was never envisaged during my parents' lifetime.

My father, however, was determined that I and my brother should get the best education possible and not be handicapped as he had been. His immediate goal was a public school, and Mill Hill was then the leading Free Church foundation. So in 1926 at the age of thirteen I secured a ministerial exhibition, the scholarship awarded to the sons of Free Church ministers. Maurice Jacks was the headmaster, appointed at the early age of twenty-seven to succeed Sir John McClure, and reputedly the rising star in the educational world. The school, however, turned out to be a far from progressive institution, at least as that is understood today. Boarders – and they constituted the great majority, the few day boys being largely ignored and treated as second class citizens – experienced a Spartan existence. There was no hot water for washing either in the morning or later in the day. The indoor swimming bath was unheated and was freezing cold even in the summer. Outdoor games took precedence over everything else and those who came back from the playing fields caked in mud washed themselves in long troughs of tepid and inevitably dirty water, sitting feet to tail, before plunging into the icy waters of the swimming bath.

The food was unappetizing. We were given a substantial mid-day meal in which the headmaster and other masters shared, but the breakfasts and high teas left much to be desired. Porridge was served in the mornings accompanied by thick slices of bread thinly coated with margerine, known as 'scrape'. To make them palatable boys had to provide their own jars of marmalade or jam. For high tea there was a rissole or slice of tinned meat with the same plentiful supply of 'scrape'. Tea was a concoction of grey liquid poured from large urns, the like of which I hope never to see again. It looked and tasted like dish water and its only redeeming features were that it was hot and wet. It was hardly surprising that we looked forward to the holidays and the welcome prospect of home food.

Mill Hill was chiefly noted for its reputation for rugby football. This was deservedly established during my first term in 1926. The first fifteen won all their matches, often with very big margins, and crowned its achievements with a notable victory over a strong side from the London Scottish. This was largely due to the outstanding ability of the fly-half and centre three-quarters, Auty, Collinson and Carris who were soon to be capped for England at Twickenham. They were succeeded shortly afterwards by the remarkable P. D. Howard who as a child had contracted polio and had broken his withered leg trying to play games as one of the new boys at the school. This was assumed to be the end of all sporting activities as far as he was concerned. However, on his recovery he started to play rugger again and with extraordinary courage he managed to secure selection to the first team where with his long, gangling stride he distinguished himself as one of the forwards. He went on to Oxford where he was awarded his 'blue' and was then selected captain of England. He became even better known as one of the leading members of the Oxford Group Movement, otherwise described as the 'Buchmanites', who came to prominence in the nineteen-thirties for promoting Moral Rearmament.

This emphasis on games meant that academic work took second place. Prowess at sports was the goal to be achieved and promotion to positions of leadership and responsibility largely depended on it. On the whole the assistant masters were not of high quality, though amongst them were real scholars such as Alan Whitehorn who taught the classical sixth. Maurice Jacks, the headmaster, was something of an enigma. He was a competent administrator, a firm disciplinarian and eminently successful in public relations; the reputation of the school stood high during his headmastership. But he was an introverted, cold, aloof personality with whom it was difficult for boys to relate except for holding him in respect. But I have never been able to understand why he was regarded as a progressive educationalist or what his students made of him or learnt from him when he left Mill Hill to become director of the Oxford School of Education. He had been responsible for what I can only describe in retrospect as the Philistine nature of the school, and his own method of teaching, even in the sixth form, was to dictate material to be laboriously copied into notebooks. I have rarely encountered a teacher less imaginative and more uninspiring. My own school career was a hard slog, unrelieved by any inspiration or stimulus in the classroom, and even in the sixth form where I spent three years under the tutelage of Alan Whitehorn, the classics never came alive for me as languages and literature of which I had got the feel. I was always labouring to secure the correct translation and sentence construction. It was only later at Oxford that learning became exciting exploration. The fault was no doubt largely mine; for Alan was capable of communicating to others his own love for the classics. But throughout my school-days I was never given the confidence that I was anything but rather stupid academically: a misfortune which could only be remedied by hard work.

To return to my early days at Mill Hill. My first year was a miserable one. New bugs, as they were called, were treated like dirt by those who had passed beyond the stage of initiation and who were determined to teach their juniors what they thought was a proper sense of inferiority and insignificance. This might not have been so bad for young upstarts, but it was frightening for the majority suddenly faced with the prospect of life beyond the familiar protection of home. New boys arrived the day before the rest to find their way about the place, but when the whole school assembled on the following afternoon they were lined up in the passage outside the common rooms and subjected to their first experience of humiliation. 'What's your name, boy? Aren't you horrid?' This was followed within the next few days by the ordeal of the new bugs' concert, delayed while the rumour was spread around of what this would entail. It consisted of being brought one by one into a common room crowded for the fun and made to stand on a table and sing a song to the jeers of the tormentors. It was made all the more terrifying by being compelled to jump around while singing to avoid the sticks which were aimed at the feet of the unfortunate victims. On the first day the monitors and prefects selected new boys to be their fags. To be chosen to perform menial duties for these high and mighty seniors turned out to be something of an advantage; for the timid new boy generally found a protector in his fag master. I was fortunate in the prefect who selected me because he was tolerant of my clumsy efforts to please. I remember being given his football boots to clean and his amused exasperation when he turned them upside down and watched the water pouring out of them!

School discipline was in the hands of the monitors, a select elite of about a dozen senior boys who had earned their promotion chiefly through their success on the playing fields. The prefects, somewhat larger in number, had limited responsibilities and were not allowed to use the swagger cane with which the monitors inflicted up to six strokes on those who were guilty of more serious offences. When anyone's name apeared on the notice board saying he was required to attend in one of the monitor's studies, he knew that a beating was in store. For minor offences up to two hundred lines or copies, as they were called, were the commonest form of punishment. This was the way discipline was maintained.

My first year under these Spartan conditions was a miserable one and I begged my father to take me away when he came to visit me during the first few weeks. How he persuaded my mother not to let him do so I have no idea, but in retrospect I believe he was right to resist my pleas. Whatever its inadequacies as an educational institution, Mill Hill provided a toughening experience for a boy who had lived a sheltered life; it developed the determination and resolution which I had inherited from my father and it had many compensations once I had survived the first year. Above everything else it enabled me to gain confidence in myself and learn not to be beaten by any obstacle.

The misery of this first year was mitigated by the school music and my growing respect for my housemaster, Victor Elliott, who with his wife Mary later became valued friends. Victor was a tall, rugged character who understood boys and whose complete integrity and unfailing fairness won their spontaneous trust. Victor had been a rugby player himself and coached the successful team of 1926. He was also the master in charge of the Shell: a form for older boys who showed no aptitude for academic work and who were thought to have no chance of securing a Higher Certificate. An old boy was once heard to remark that if so many promising sportsmen landed up in the Shell, he wondered what use there was for all the other forms! After I had left, Victor became Senior Master and was the stabilizing influence during the disastrous headmastership of Jacks's successor who managed to set the whole school, masters and boys, at loggerheads with him and there was nearly open revolt. Many years afterwards Victor told me that one day he had heard that the next morning every boy planned to go into assembly armed with a gym shoe which at a given signal they were going to fling at the headmaster when he appeared on the platform. Realizing that this was a crisis and would lead to the total breakdown of discipline, Victor went into the assembly and stood at the back, glaring at the rows of boys with their gym shoes. Such was the moral authority of his presence that not a boy dared to lift a finger and the immediate crisis passed, though the governors had to get rid of the head to avoid any further trouble. When I asked Victor what he would have done if the plot had been carried out, he replied that he hadn't the least idea. But with him there, the prospect of that happening was unthinkable. It has always seemed to me that this is the best example I know of the power of moral authority. Victor was a remarkable man.

Music, above everything else, mitigated the unhappiness of my first year. I was endowed with a good treble voice and I immediately found a place in the school choir. Membership was entirely voluntary, one of the few non-compulsory activities, but nobody dreamt of missing one of the four weekly practices if they could possibly help it. This was due to the infectious enthusiasm of Laurie Cane, the music master. He managed to enrol between fifty and a hundred boys into the choir and we enjoyed every minute of the practices. He also arranged a performance of Gilbert and Sullivan's *Trial by Jury* and I was cast in the role of the bride. When the costumes arrived it was found that my feet were too big for the shoes provided and to 'Chark's' amusement I had to wear plimsoles instead. The performance was only a qualified success, but it gave a boost to my confidence which was much needed.

After my voice broke I remained in the choir and Chark decided to try a more ambitious Gilbert and Sullivan opera. This was *H.M.S. Pinafore* and I was chosen for the part of Ralph Rackstraw. That was to give Richard Dimbleby, who was my under-study, the opportunity for his first public appearance. Two days before the performance I went down with mumps and Richard took my place. Nobody at that time would ever have dreamt that he was going to become famous as the doyen and pioneer of British broadcasters. As a boy he had great charm, but he never made the slightest effort either at work or games. His one idea seemed to be to get through the school with as little trouble as he could, and I remember him sitting in his study chair, his ample frame surrounded with cushions, blithely avoiding anything that would interfere with his comfort.

Richard became the first pianist of a group of singers which Mary Elliott organized called 'The School House Savoyards'. This met in her drawing room for practices and she drilled us in the part songs, solos and duets from all the Gilbert and Sullivan operas until she was satisfied that we were ready for concert performances. She had a lovely soprano voice and sang some of the chief parts herself. In my last year I had the privilege of playing opposite her Josephine as Admiral Sir Joseph Porter in another performance of *H.M.S. Pinafore*. That was counted a great success and I owe to her and Laurie Cane my introduction to choral and solo singing.

In my fifth year I was appointed a prefect. By then I had gained confidence, made friends and had settled down to the routine of school life. I never achieved much success at games, attaining nothing better than the captaincy of the third fifteen in rugger and captain of the fourth eleven in cricket. The latter was great fun because its membership consisted of senior boys who did not take the game too seriously and played it in a light-hearted manner, everyone, including the wicket keeper, taking turns to bowl a couple of overs. Our delight was to beat the young professionals or Colts of the third eleven whose aim was to reach the first team in due course. For my final year I was made a monitor and enjoyed the responsibilities and privileges that went with it.

In the autumn term of that year I entered for the scholarship examination at Worcester College, Oxford. My classics were not good enough for any hope of success, but Worcester was in the Balliol group and this enabled me to secure entrance to the college of my first choice as it enjoyed such a prestigious academic reputation. My admission to Balliol fulfilled my father's highest ambition and set my feet on the road to opportunities which will be the subject of the rest of this book.

Chapter Three

OXFORD

OXFORD AND BALLIOL were an entirely new world. The college's famous reputation was enhanced by what was probably the most distinguished Senior Common Room in the University. Sandy Lindsay was the Master, later to become the founder and first Vice-Chancellor of the University of North Staffordshire at Keele. Amongst the fellows were Cyril Bailey, the public orator and authority on Lucretius, and Roger Mynors, subsequently to become Professor of Classics at Cambridge. Charles Morris and John Fulton were the philosophy tutors, the former destined to be the Vice-Chancellor of Leeds and the latter the founder of the University of Sussex. F. F. Urquhart and Kenneth Bell, an eccentric genius, were the historians, Sir Harold Hartley and Ronnie Bell the scientists and Tom Pym the chaplain, whose influence on the college and on students throughout the university could scarcely be measured. Tom had been a successful athlete in his youth, but by the time I entered Balliol he had become the victim of disseminated sclerosis and being unable to handle the chalice at communion had to secure someone from outside to help him. His courage made a lasting impression on me and many others; I remember one of the undergraduates discussing some problem that seemed intractable saying to the others, 'Of course, Tom's a saint'.

The relationship with these and the other dons was completely different from anything to which I had been accustomed with the masters at school. They treated us as adults and expected us to be on friendly terms with them. One of my earliest experiences of this was in my first term. I had been assigned a room on Dicey which was situated high up on the third floor of a staircase in the garden quad. After breakfast one morning there was a knock at my door and the senior tutor, F. F. Urquhart, affectionately known as 'Sligger', came into the room. He collapsed into an armchair, completely out of breath from the effort of climbing three flights of stairs. He had an acute heart condition from which he was shortly to die after a lifetime's care and friendship for successive generations of undergraduates. When he had recovered his breath he said, 'Your old headmaster is coming to lunch with me today and I wondered whether you would like to join us'. I was completely taken aback by the kindness of the invitation and the unnecessary trouble he had taken to deliver it. He could easily have sent me a note by one of the college servants, but he wanted to offer the invitation himself. I learnt that this was typical of him, but that he should have taken all this trouble over a raw freshman made a lasting impression upon me. It was a courtesy from an older man such as I had not experienced before and was striking evidence of the new world I had entered.

On another occasion I received an invitation to dinner in the old Senior Common Room by Kenneth Bell. The card told us that this was to be a black tie affair, and we duly assembled at the time appointed to find the college silver laid out on the table and a sumptuous dinner served by the scouts, the college servants, on duty. The small group of undergraduates were mystified by the question why they had been asked to such a feast, but we were soon to learn. When dinner was over Kenneth invited us into the adjoining room for coffee and port.

Then he stood in front of the fire and said, 'You are no doubt wondering why I have invited you to dinner tonight. The reason is that the other day one of the members of this college passed another in the quad without saying "Good morning". Manners today are terrible. You do not even know how to reply to an invitation. I had all kinds of answers such as "Mr Smith has much pleasure in accepting the kind invitation of Mr Kenneth Bell to dinner on such and such a date!" Don't you know that the correct way of replying is to answer in exactly the same terms as the invitation? I addressed you by your Christian names and I expected you to answer "Dear Kenneth" and end "Yours ever Joe"!' The dinner must have cost him a lot, but this eccentricity endeared him to those who were present and was a surprising way of introducing us to a different kind of relationship with the dons from anything we had expected.

I had entered the school of Classical Honour Moderations: a course which covered the whole of Latin and Greek literature. My tutors were Cyril Bailey and Roger Mynors and given such renowned and stimulating supervision I should have done far better than I did. But I was still dogged by the way I had approached my school work in the past and the freedom of being left to study on my own and choose what lectures I wished to attend was a totally new experience to which I took a long time to adjust. In the end my pedestrian efforts led only to a third class in the spring of 1934.

A year before that my father had been inducted into the Presidency of the Baptist Union of Great Britain and Ireland at the annual assembly in Glasgow. He chose as the subject of his address the place of women in the ministry of the church, based on his experience of partnership with my mother and the mixed staff of the West Ham Central Mission in which women predominated. That day the *Glasgow Evening News* carried as the banner headline on the front page, 'Women Revolt Against The Church', anticipating today's controversy about the ordination of women by over half a century. I would have liked to have been there, but my father dissuaded me from coming lest it would interfere with my course at Oxford. This was another instance of his concern that my education should take precedence over everything else.

In the Trinity or summer term of 1934 I embarked on Literae Humaniores, commonly referred to as 'Greats', then regarded as the most demanding intellectual course at Oxford. It was divided between philosophy and ancient history and opened up new and exciting horizons for me. I attended a seminar conducted by Professor R. G. Collingwood and lectures by H. H. Price and Gilbert Ryle. These began to stimulate my interest in philosophy which was to become my specialized subject. I also went to Professor H. A. Prichard's lectures on moral philosophy. He was a wizened little man who perched himself on a bench behind the lectern at Oriel and enthusiastically hunted down utilitarians as if they were a bunch of rats. His invariable practice was ruthlessly to analyse the work of the principal authorities on the subject, claiming that if they meant what they said they were obviously confused and therefore talking nonsense.

One day I was rash enough to ask him a question at the end of his lecture. He said he had not time to answer it then, but if I would give him my name and college he would invite me to come to his house and discuss it. In due course a note arrived setting a time for me to go and see him. On the appointed evening I knocked on the door and the great man opened it himself. He sat me down on one side of the fireplace in his drawing room and seated himself in the armchair opposite. Then he asked me what was my question. I cannot remember what it was, but I left over an hour later having been convinced that there was not a single word in my question the meaning of which I had understood! That put the devil in me and from that moment I pursued the subject with enthusiasm. To Prichard's kindness and rigorous criticism I owe more than I can say.

Another remarkable lecturer in Greats was Marcus Tod of Oriel. He was the most distinguished epigraphist of his day and it was said of him that when, after taking his finals as an undergraduate, he went for his viva, the examiners rose to their feet, took off their mortarboards and simply said 'Thank you, Mr Tod'. His use of language was pedantic in the extreme. I recall that at the beginning of the first lecture I attended he made the following request: 'Will gentlemen kindly open the left hand leaf of the door as well as the right hand leaf of the door at the end of the lecture in order to facilitate the egress!' His lectures were meticulously prepared and delivered word for word from the text in front of him. They were carefully timed to last exactly the allotted fifty minutes. On one occasion he found that he had still got several sentences left in his manuscript when the time came for him to finish. In some confusion he explained that he would have to leave the remainder of what he had to say to the beginning of the next lecture. The following week he began where he had left off, but after a couple of minutes, to the amusement of his audience, he said, 'In the minute or two that remain I ...'. He blushed to the roots of his hair when everybody burst out laughing.

On another occasion he indulged in what was for him a completely uncharacteristic and unscripted aside. He frequently referred to the distinguished American epigraphists, Merritt and West. On this occasion he quoted West without reference to Merritt saying, 'You may be surprised that I refer in this connection to Professor West without mentioning Professor Merritt. You have doubtless come to think of them both as you do of – er – Laurel and Hardy'. Even if we were not particularly interested in what he had to say about Greek inscriptions, it was a delight to listen to him and await some outrageously pedantic sentence.

In my last year I had the inestimable privilege of being tutored by Charles Morris. We were accustomed to go each week for tutorials in pairs, one to read an essay on alternate weeks and the other to comment upon it. Charles usually listened in silence until his pupil had finished reading; then he would stare into the fire, sometimes for two or three minutes, before turning suddenly upon the reader's companion with the question, 'What did you think about what he said about so and so in the middle of his paper?' Then the devastating criticism would begin. The probably apocryphal story is told that two girl students from Somerville were farmed out on him for tutorials, but on this occasion one of them was ill and the other had to come alone. She read a particularly brilliant essay after which Charles stared into the fire for some time.

Suddenly he whipped round and said, 'Will you marry me?' That, it was said, is how he came to marry Lady Morris, herself a distinguished philosopher. Whether the story is apocryphal or not, it rings true as far as my memory of his stimulating tutorials is concerned. His criticism was meticulous and devastating. You were not allowed to get away with a muddled idea or a slipshod piece of writing. To Charles Morris, as to H. A. Prichard, I owe my determination to avoid woolly thinking and seek for clarity and conciseness in expression. Many years later I was grateful to be able to pay tribute to him in the preface of a book on a philosophical approach to theology, entitled *Interpreting Human Experience* which was published by Collins in 1971.

My Roman history tutor was 'Topes' Stone, a real eccentric living alone in rooms on the top floor above the Oriel restaurant in High street. Reputedly he never left them in daylight; at least I never saw him outside those rooms nor did I meet anyone who had. He is said to have written a book on metaphysics which he showed to the Master. When he had read it, Sandy Lindsay is reported to have told him that he did not understand it. Whereupon Topes rewrote it and sent it back to the Master, who this time commented that although he had found the original manuscript obscure, he could not make any sense whatever out of the revision! Whether that is true or not, Topes's real subject was Roman history and in this he was a brilliant tutor.

He suffered not only from acute shyness but also from total deafness and his pupils could only communicate with him in writing. But he lived in Roman history and spoke as if he knew the principal characters intimately. I remember him once saying, 'People wonder why Caesar crossed the Rubicon. The answer is really quite simple: he loved killing Gauls!' He made copious notes on the essays you left with him and then when you went back for a tutorial he would discourse brilliantly on the subject, striding up and down the room as he did so. I had put all my eggs in the philosophy basket and did not expect to do any better in Ancient History than secure reasonable marks in the final examination to support the philosophy papers. But such was the fascination of Topes's tutorials that in the final examination I secured a mark in Roman history which was on the borderline of first class.

Charles Morris told me that he expected me to get a first on the strength of my philosophy, but in the event I just failed to do so. I think I had waked up too late academically. Nevertheless, Charles sent me an encouraging note enclosing my marks which gave me the stimulus to follow up the questions arising from my work in Greats.

But Balliol was not only academically rewarding; we had ample opportunity to pursue other interests. I had caught something of my uncle's enthusiasm for soccer and at Oxford I was able to take up the game which I had been prevented from doing before because only rugger was played at Mill Hill. I kept goal for the college eleven and in my final year we distinguished ourselves by getting through four rounds of 'cuppers', beating Jesus, Pembroke, New College and St Peter's Hall to reach the final on the Iffley Road ground. There we met Brasenose, generally known as B.N.C., a team which consisted of more than one blue and an amateur international. But we lost only narrowly by four goals to three. That was the only occasion on which I featured in the sporting pages of *The Times*. The reporter simply recorded that 'the goalkeeper was sadly at fault' and later that 'the goalkeeper was again sadly at fault'. We would have won if it had not been for my fumbling, but

Raymond Saunders, the captain, was indulgently forgiving and we went out together for the evening, more for a wake than a celebration. He was a close friend and later became chief education officer for Worcestershire.

Singing in the Oxford Bach choir was a constant source of pleasure. The chorus numbered about 400 and it was a challenge to be able to tackle major works such as Bach's Mass in B Minor. Rehearsals were held in the Ashmolean Museum with W. H. Harris and later Sir Thomas Armstrong as conductors. The basses from Balliol used to sit with Cyril Bailey who invited us to The Mound, his house in Mansfield Road, for extra practices. For one or more concerts Sir Hugh Allen was invited as guest conductor. He delighted in being outrageously rude to choir and orchestra during rehearsals and everybody loved it. Our accompanist was an excellent pianist, but she too was the butt of his mischief. On one occasion we were rehearsing the great chorus 'Behold all flesh is as the grass' from Brahms' Requiem when suddenly, with a wicked twinkle in his eye, Sir Hugh threw down his baton and exclaimed, 'You can't play the piano'. Looking up at the back row of the basses at Dykes Bower, who was later to become organist at St Paul's Cathedral and was then at New College, he said, 'Dykes Bower, come down and show her how to play it'. Dykes Bower, with the full score of the music in front of him, accompanied the choir with such brilliance that everybody stopped singing and burst into applause. Sir Hugh glowered down at him and growled, 'Dykes Bower, where are the drums?' Later at the final rehearsal when the whole orchestra was crowded into the confined space of the practice room, the same chorus was in full blast. Again Sir Hugh cried 'Stop'. Turning to an unfortunate girl at the last desk of the first violins, he said, 'My good young woman, you might as well be playing that fiddle with a banana for all the good you are doing!' You never knew what he was going to say next, but the uncertainty and anticipation added immeasurably to the joy of sitting under him.

In my last year at Mill Hill I applied for admission to Regent's Park College for training for the ministry after I should have completed my undergraduate course at Oxford. This involved sitting a preliminary examination on the Bible. The report on how I had done was given me by the senior tutor, A. J. Farrer, the father of Austen Farrer, the well-known Oxford philosopher. I was a somewhat nervous teenager who was far from sure of his ground and I thought I had better get in a word of explanation first. 'I'm afraid, sir, I don't know much about the prophets.' 'That's putting it rather mildly, Mr Clifford', said Farrer dryly. All the same I was accepted and given a bursary to help pay my fees at Balliol.

Regent's Park College had by then abandoned its imposing building in the park and the students combined with those of the Congregational New College in North London. But the Principal, Dr H. Wheeler Robinson, was determined that the Baptists should establish a college of their own in Oxford. The other Free Churches had foundations at one of the two major universities, the Congregationalists at Mansfield in Oxford, the Presbyterians and Methodists in Cambridge at Westminster and Wesley House respectively. There were some people who believed the time had come to forego distinctively denominational training and that Baptists should combine with the Congregationalists at Mansfield. But that was to anticipate the policy which happily began to be put into effect after the war, notably with the establishment of The Queen's College in Birmingham as a fully ecumenical institution. At any rate Wheeler thought otherwise and he persuaded his council to acquire a large house in St Giles where he would live and make plans for building on the adjoining land in Pusey Street.

At the time, therefore, when I went to Balliol some of the students continued to study at New College in London, while those who were thought capable of sitting for the Honours School of Theology at Oxford were admitted to the Junior Common Room at

Mansfield while preserving their identity by meeting at 55, St Giles for seminars and tutorials under Wheeler Robinson and his assistant, Leonard Brockington. Accordingly, during my time at Balliol I was treated as a student of Regent's Park and was encouraged to attend college luncheons at the Cadena Cafe every week.

After I had taken my finals I joined the Regent's men at Mansfield for the next two years. During the first week we were required to write papers on the main subjects of the theological curriculum, designed to show how far we were advanced in them before we embarked on the course. These were handed back with comments at a formal meeting presided over by Dr Nathaniel Micklem, the Principal of Mansfield, with the rest of the dons of both colleges sitting on either side of the table. Nath sat at one end and the student opposite to him. He had read my paper on the philosophy of religion and he took the opportunity of taking me down a peg. 'You Greats men', he remarked, 'never seem to know that any philosophy was written after Plato and Aristotle until the time of Descartes. Haven't you ever heard of St Thomas Aquinas?' Wheeler was clearly disconcerted. I was the first man he had who had read Greats and he was sensitive to any criticism that Nath might offer; there was always evident tension between them. 'I think you had better go to tutorials with Dr Micklem on St Thomas', said Wheeler. This turned out to be just the right thing for me; Nath was a most stimulating scholar and from then onwards he became my beloved mentor.

As I had already taken an honours degree, I was not entered for the school of theology, but was allowed to prepare for the qualifying examination for the Oxford BD. This gave me the freedom to pursue my own interests and enabled me to spend a disproportionate amount of time working under Nathaniel Micklem. Many years afterwards, when I returned from Canada, Nath invited me to join the All Souls Club over which he presided.

This was a small dining club which met three times a year in London, the members taking it in turns to act as host and read a paper which was discussed until ten o'clock when Nath would take out his watch and bring the proceedings to a close. It was formed after the First World War and consisted of an equal number of Anglo-Catholics and Free Churchmen, clerical and lay, and amongst its founders were T. S. Eliot, Harold Darke and Lord Selbourne. When I joined Lord Reith was a member until the time of his death and later Archbishop Michael Ramsey, Dr Eric Mascall, Dr John Huxtable and Sir Robert Birley were among those who participated. The papers were always stimulating and I particularly remember the occasion when Nath himself was our host and at nearly eighty years of age delivered a paper on how to commend the Christian Faith to an agnostic without using any of the traditional theological language. Frailty finally compelled him to resign. His last visitor was Michael Ramsey who told the next meeting of the club that Nath's was the most Christian death he had ever encountered. 'He looked up at me and said "I'm neither here nor there; I'm only just in between".' It was ultimately my privilege to succeed Nath as secretary, and the membership had by then been extended to Roman Catholics, Orthodox and women, notable amongst whom was Rosalind Goodfellow, the first woman Moderator of the United Reformed Church.

To digress for a moment. Nath's father was also called Nathaniel and was chairman of the governors of Mill Hill while I was there. He lived to the great age of a hundred and was a QC in two reigns – those of Victoria and the present Queen. When Nath retired from the principalship of Mansfield, his father is reported to have said, 'Drat it! I thought I had got the boy settled!' He showed a proper sense of proportion on his deathbed when his last two questions were 'Is the cherry tree in bloom?' and 'What is the test match score?' Nath must have inherited from his father this sense of priorities, for he could never take himself or anyone else too seriously and the twinkle in his eye was rarely absent. His own son also became a barrister like his grandfather and was christened Nath and in turn produced another Nath who was the delight of his own father in his old age.

Returning to my own two years at Regent's, it was customary for the men to be assigned to student pastorates in village churches to give them some practical experience during the course of preparation for the ministry. By the mid nineteen-thirties my father had become exhausted. He was nearly seventy years of age and the invitation to a senior Baptist minister to join him as a colleague and take some of the burden off his shoulders had not been a success. David Tait Patterson was a highly regarded and able minister, but he and my father were temperamentally incompatible. It would have been extremely difficult anyway for a senior man with the experience of ploughing his own furrow to adjust to someone who had spent all his life in the ministry in one place. When Tait Patterson felt he had to leave, what was to be done? There seemed to be only one solution and Wheeler Robinson was persuaded to let me become student assistant to my father. This meant travelling up to London every weekend on Saturday mornings and returning to Oxford by the last train on Sunday nights. Thus I found myself tied to West Ham while still at Oxford, but I have never regretted it; it gave me the unique opportunity of taking on heavy responsibilities at a very early age and opened doors to so much that lay ahead.

Throughout my six years at Oxford religion was a live issue. With my evangelical background I naturally joined the Inter-Collegiate Christian Union which seemed to be the liveliest and most influential Christian organization in the university. But as time passed the atmosphere of the OICCU became increasingly constrictive. I soon found biblical fundamentalism wholly unsatisfactory and larger horizons were opening up before me. One of my Balliol friends, Ian Thomson, organized a large rally in Oxford Town Hall with the striking, if somewhat pretentious slogan, 'Can Oxford Believe in Jesus Christ?' Ian had great charm. He rowed in the record-breaking Oxford boat and was highly regarded not only in his own college, but throughout the university. On the night appointed the Town Hall was crowded with undergraduates and some of the most prominent personalities in the university were on the platform. It was a bold and memorable venture.

The Student Christian Movement was also in its heyday and William Temple, then Archbishop of York was a regular visitor and a power in the land. When he came to preach at St Mary's the church was crowded to capacity, with students sitting in the aisles and on the chancel steps eager to hear what he had to say. One of his memorable 'bon mots' was when he said, 'There are some people who seem to think that what I believe is due to the way I was held as a baby. My reply to them is that what they believe about me is due to the way they were held as babies!' I remember him processing up the aisle in his voluminous robes – on a visit to Switzerland his surplice was once returned from the laundry marked 'One bell tent' – and ascending the small, high pulpit with his robes touchimg it all the way round. He reminded one of an oversized egg in an egg-cup! But his sermons had a lasting influence on those who were privileged to listen to him.

Those were great days and, with C. S. Lewis in his prime, the impact of Christianity on the university was destined to be far-reaching. Thus I came down from Oxford with my faith strengthened and confirmed and with high hopes for the future.

Chapter Four

WEST HAM IN WAR-TIME

I WAS ORDAINED to the Christian ministry by Dr Wheeler Robinson in the Memorial Church of the West Ham Central Mission on September 25th 1938. The building was crowded for the service and it was an inspiring start to a young man's ministry. In spite of the difficulties to which I referred in the previous chapter, the Mission had continued to expand in the pre-war years. The church was packed every Monday afternoon for the service for women which my mother invariably led, though visiting speakers from nearly every Christian denomination gave the address. There was always a soloist and leading artistes in the musical world such as Stiles Allen, Elsie Suddaby, Isobel Baillie, Muriel Brunskill and many others were glad to offer their services. Most notable among them was Dame Clara Butt who had presented the fine organ named after her. She was a great friend of the Mission and when she died my father gave the address at her memorial service in All Souls, Langham Place, and our scouts, of which she was the patron, formed the guard of honour.

However, the main feature of the service on Monday afternoons was the notices given out by my mother. These could last for anything up to half an hour and consisted of a review of everything that had been happening during the week in the district and the world at large. This was like playing a violin. Such was my mother's rapport with the vast congregation that what she said would evoke murmurs of approval or consternation as the case might be. She was endowed with a remarkable speaking voice and every word could easily be heard in the farthest corners of the large building, and that without the aid of modern methods of amplification. There is no doubt that throughout these pre-war

42

years this Monday afternoon service was the most remarkable feature of the Mission, and the twenty-fifth anniversary of its inception was celebrated by a second visit by Queen Mary in 1930.

My father and mother with Hugh and myself, 1941

But there had been other developments. The old Tabernacle was no longer needed for Sunday services and the imaginative idea was conceived of turning it into a church for children. The basement hall was shored up with steel girders, the pews removed from the main concourse and a floor was constructed to span the circle of the gallery to form a new chapel for worship. This was a radical departure from the old type of Sunday school: a church for boys and girls under fifteen years of age with three floors: one for play, one for work in clubs and one for worship.

Adjoining the new church up the road, a Hall of Youth was built with facilities for a gymnasium; homes for the elderly were opened, and a timber yard next to the Settlement House was acquired and turned into a garden with nursery school premises erected beside the gate. With all these developments centred around a living church of about a thousand members, many saw it as leading the way to a more effective ministry to the deprived areas of our inner cities. This was the exciting prospect which confronted me when I took up my responsibilities at West Ham.

But the clouds of war were gathering on the horizon and it was already beginning to become apparent that the old paternalistic approach would have to be abandoned and the Mission would have to adapt to entirely new conditions. Nevertheless, the time was not yet ripe for radical change and for that first year I was left to become established and to take stock of what had to be done.

Then the inevitable happened. The growing threat of Nazi aggression led to the invasion of Poland and Neville Chamberlain was driven to declare that we were at war with Germany in a broadcast to the British people on that memorable Sunday morning of September 3rd 1939. The sirens sounded as the congregation was joining in worship and the service was suspended to allow people to take shelter in the passages behind the church and underneath the galleries. Everyone expected a mass raid on London and the holocaust of war bursting upon the capital, but the imminent threat of devastation did not, of course, materialize. However, the sense of shock remained and as people made their way home they realized that within the past few hours life had radically changed.

The first weeks of the 'twilight war' as it was called did not seriously affect the people of West Ham. The children were evacuated, but except for some of the more carefully organized parties, like our own nursery school and its staff, most drifted back when the threat of air raids failed to materialize. The 'call-up' affected comparatively few and life went on much as usual. In a dock district, of course, there were many families who had men at sea, and as ships began to be sunk there were casualties; but only a home here and there was affected. Then on November 23rd came the news of the sinking of the armed cruiser *Rawalpindi* with the loss of her captain and 270 of the crew. Only 38 survived, 27 of

The Ministerial Team at the outbreak of war:
Bill Bodey, Denis Lant, my father and myself

whom were taken prisoners. This was a terrible blow to the district, for the ship was largely manned by men from the neighbourhood and many families connected with us were bereaved. On the following Monday afternoon a Remembrance service was held for the large congregation of women who thronged the church. Many came that day dressed in black, evidence of how stricken the district had been.

The disaster in Norway and the fall of Chamberlain's government brought the first realization that, so far, we hardly knew what war was. The invasion of the Low Countries, the evacuation from Dunkirk and the fall of France followed in quick and bewildering succession. The beginning of serious hostilities gave rise to a second evacuation of children from the district and the schools were closed. Many parents, however, would not allow their children to go, preferring to take the risk of keeping them at home. The result was that numbers of boys and girls were roaming the streets with nothing to do except get into mischief. We decided to open our own school in the Children's Church. My brother was then at Balliol and the summer vacation had just begun. So he organized a group of Oxford students to come and conduct the classes. Our impromptu school was a great success while it lasted, but within a week the authorities had decided to bow to the inevitable and the ordinary schools were reopened. But the effort had not been wasted. We had learned how to improvise in meeting an unexpected emergency and we had made contact with undergraduates at Oxford who, with many of their friends, were to render invaluable service when the blitz burst upon us in all its fury.

Towards the end of August it was clear that the long-expected air raids were at last imminent. The battle of Britain had begun. The problem of providing shelters for the crowded population of West Ham was a formidable one. Many of the houses had been built on marsh land, and this meant that any structure underground was liable to be flooded. Consequently there were scarcely any cellars available and even the specially constructed Anderson shelters provided for families above the ground were difficult to keep dry and usable. The bottom floor of the Children's Church was a rare exception. It was partly underground and, when the building was altered, the weight of the roof and the floors had been supported by huge steel stanchions. The Local Authority had earlier earmarked the basement floor as a public air raid shelter, and we had offered to man it with our own personnel.

Then on Saturday afternoon September 8th the attack began. At the Children's Church a party was being held for nearly 200 boys and girls with the help of a group of students from Oxford. When the sirens sounded the children were shepherded to the basement and passers-by were admitted; but no one had anticipated the fury of the onslaught. Over 500 bombers launched a mass attack on the docks, and the little houses in the crowded streets suffered fearful damage. As we emerged from the shelters after the sounding of the 'All clear' the sky was blotted out by a pall of smoke; the air reeked with the fumes of gelignite and the whole district was ringed with a circle of flame. It seemed that we were in the middle of hell's inferno.

That night the bombers returned to stoke up the fires and they came back again and again, night after night. The shelter at the Children's Church was packed almost to suffocation. Our scoutmaster, Fred Beagles, a giant of a man, was in charge and it needed his tremendous physique and powerful voice to hold the crowd through that first night of terror. Thereafter he took it in turns with me to be responsible for the packed shelter every night while the raids lasted.

For the first twenty-four hours the main church buildings escaped damage, but in the early hours of Monday morning a heavy bomb exploded at the end of the adjoining garden. My father and mother, with the members of the staff who were not on duty at the Children's Church, spent the night in the tiny boiler room of the main church, lying on mattresses covering the surface of the floor, while the old caretaker occupied the corner by the entrance. As we emerged into the early morning light a scene of destruction and devastation greeted us. Most of the windows in the Settlement House and the Hall of Youth were broken; the roof had been blown off the men's club, and the old people's home, fortunately evacuated, looked a shambles. The garden was strewn with rubble; the houses at the end were wrecked and the Nursery School building damaged beyond repair. As my mother surveyed the sight in the half-light of dawn she turned to me and said, 'All our life's work gone'. So it seemed on that bleak September morning.

But the damage to buildings could be repaired. People were far more important and we were to discover the emergence of a new church life from the ruins which seemed so devastating. Many of our people were scattered; the children were evacuated; normal activities had to be suspended; and even church services had to be curtailed since it was impossible to meet after dusk. Nevertheless, a faithful remnant was left including many of our best leaders and we had a splendid staff, supplemented by university students. The need of the district was clamant and in facing it the life of the Mission had a new beginning.

When air raids were first envisaged, the authorities thought in terms of short, sharp attacks with heavy casualties. Preparations were made accordingly and there was ample provision to deal with the dead and injured. Happily, in spite of the widespread nature of the attacks, the casualties were comparatively few. No one, however, had foreseen the problem of the homeless and the unnerved. For every single person killed or injured there were fifty or even a hundred in desperate need of assistance. In the face of this the public administrative arrangements broke down. That was nobody's fault. The scale and nature of the problem could hardly have been envisaged in advance. It was a case for improvisation and emergency measures.

We had an experienced staff, equipment and resources which could be devoted at once to meeting the needs as they arose. Moreover, 'The Tab' was known and loved and it quickly became a centre to which people looked for help. The first thing to be tackled was the shelter problem. Queues lined up in the late afternoon to secure admission for the night; mothers carried bundles in their arms with their most precious possessions; children and old people waited hopefully for a chance to get inside. Officially we were supposed to provide space for a maximum of 200 and that assessment had been made on the assumption that air raids would last only twenty minutes or half an hour. We were faced with the difficulty of accommodating as many as we could for twelve, thirteen and fourteen hours at a stretch. In those early days we could not restrict numbers to 200; we had to crowd in as many as we possibly could and we somehow found room for up to 500.

Gradually order emerged out of chaos. A children's corner was set aside and furnished for the young ones and volunteers acted as nurses at night. Bunks were installed and blankets provided for every shelterer. The men formed themselves into a fire guard for the building and kept watch in shifts throughout the night. Canteen facilities were made available for those who had to come straight from work, and morning and evening prayers were led by the member of staff on duty. Old hymns and prayers took on new meaning, as with the collect, 'Lighten our darkness we beseech thee, O Lord, and by thy great mercy defend us from all perils and dangers of the night for the love of thy only Son, our Saviour, Jesus Christ'. With reverence and simple trust this mixed family entered into the act of worship; for a family it soon became, as close knit a community as many had ever experienced.

As the weeks went by life became centred around the activities of this underground community. Concerts and sing-songs passed

49

many an anxious hour, and the cockney cheerfulness and humour soon came to the surface. An old character known as Bill was a familiar and beloved figure. He must have weighed nearly eighteen stones and his face was always wreathed in smiles. When a particularly heavy bomb crashed down nearby, someone was sure to cry out: 'It's all right; Uncle Bill's fallen out of his bunk!' A burst of laughter would follow, quieting unsteady nerves.

Every Sunday night a service was held in the shelter. Among the vivid memories is the evening when this service was broadcast by the BBC with a mobile anti-aircraft gun blazing away in the street outside. The commentator described the scene: the nurses in their uniforms, the children in their corner and the members of this strange community perched on the top of their bunks.

The shelter at the Children's Church soon became a centre of service to the neighbourhood. Each night, after the sirens had sounded and the bombs had begun to fall, parties set out by car and van to the notorious arches under the Silvertown Way, to trench and surface shelters and to as many places as possible where people were taking refuge. Two huge coppers in the kitchen, installed at the time of the Silvertown explosion in the First World War, provided hot soup and cocoa which were conveyed in thermostatic urns. In this way about 1000 hot drinks were served every night to many shelterers all over the district. The squads, in their tin helmets, carried the urns with trays of buns to the people who had to spend all those hours under protective covering, and the arrival of the party with the mobile canteen was always eagerly welcomed.

In the early days of the blitz sanitary conditions in the shelters left everything to be desired and those who were forced to spend long hours crowded together, often in damp quarters and breathing an atmosphere that could be cut with a knife, were open to the ravages of infectious disease and all kinds of ailment. It was remarkable that there was no epidemic. After the first two or three weeks a mobile squad was formed, led by Red Cross nurses, one of them only nineteen years of age. There was no properly equipped vehicle for the purpose and a borrowed car had to serve. Night after night these girls went out with their first-aid box, giving what help they could and, by their cheerful efficiency, carrying with them a spirit of confidence to all with whom they came in contact. Later the American Committee for Air Raid Relief gave us a van which was euphemistically called an ambulance and nicknamed 'Blanche'. The larger space enabled others to accompany the nurses, prepared, wherever possible, to hold a concert or a sing-song. I remember one night in the shelter under the arches in the Silvertown Way when I was trying to organize a concert in one of the small bays for which bunks had by then been provided. Two girls were sitting on one of the lower bunks and I suggested that they might be prepared to sing. 'Only if you'll give us a mike' was the reply: a request totally unnecessary in the confined space. For the first time I realized that a generation was growing up which had never heard anyone singing except through a microphone, which may go far to explain why so many speakers and actors today are inaudible when left without mechanical aids.

While the needs of the shelterers made a special claim upon the personnel and resources at our disposal, there were many other urgent problems to be faced. Every morning as dawn broke a carload of members of the staff set out for the streets where there had been incidents. This was known as 'doing damage': a somewhat strange expression to describe what was actually accomplished! The homes of the adherents of the Mission had to be visited and comfort and advice given to those who looked to us for help. Then there were the many others who faced the loss of their possessions and the breaking-up of their accustomed life. Before many months had passed there were few who had not experienced what it meant to be 'bombed out' and for an increasing number this had happened two, three and four times.

At first no official provision was made for evacuating any others than children of school age, those with children under five, and expectant mothers. The plight of the aged, the invalids and the unnerved was pitiable in the extreme. During the first weeks of serious bombing an appeal was made to churches in safe areas to receive parties of those who could not leave London under one of the officially sponsored schemes and the response was both immediate and generous. But this involved considerable problems of organization. My first secretary, Dorothy White, was given the task of setting up an office on the middle floor of the Children's Church to deal with the situation. Incidentally, I mention her by name here because she will feature in surprising circumstances at the end of this autobiography, but more of that later. With a number of assistants she met the challenge with great efficiency and within a very short time well over 1000 had been found new homes through this improvised office.

Many more wanted advice on all kinds of questions: how to make claims for war damage; where to get clothes to replace those they had lost; how to find money for their fare to a friend's home or to a billet that had been offered them. In the eight months from September 1940 to May 1941 over 6000 people passed through the middle floor of the Children's Church to be interviewed by members of the staff and other volunteers.

Between three and four thousand were completely reclothed during the same period. It is difficult now to imagine what that involved: men, women and children of all shapes and sizes requiring new outfits and changes of garments. The clothing store became a fitting-room and the Hall of Youth was turned into a great depot with piles of dresses, suits, coats, undergarments and shoes. An army of volunteers undertook sorting and stacking, as the bales from America, Canada and all over the world were delivered and unpacked. The capacity of the gymnasium was taxed to the uttermost and the piles of clothing almost reached the ceiling.

The Mission staff was not adequate to meet the challenge unaided. A large number of members of the church came forward to take their share of responsibility in mobile squads, in the shelter, in the canteen, in the clothing store and wherever else they were required. Their number was supplemented during the Christmas vacation of 1940 by nearly forty dons and students from Oxford, many of whom encountered the church in action for the first time and ultimately became influential leaders in the Church at large. This turned out to be one of the most significant outcomes of those grim days even if we did not fully appreciate it at the time. But more of this in the next chapter.

In the meanwhile one of the younger members of the ministerial team, Bill Bodey, with his wife Gladys took charge of Child Haven, the home the Mission had acquired in Shenfield. It was wonderful to have this centre in the comparative safety of Essex to which mothers and children could be sent away from the scenes of destruction. During the five years of war in which the Bodeys were in charge of Child Haven 1100 children, over 400 mothers and approximately the same number of babies were welcomed, cared for and restored to health.

During the early months of 1941 there was comparative relief from heavy raiding. The crowds continued to come to the shelters and the problems of the homeless remained. Then on two successive nights, May 10th and 11th, the full fury of the attack was launched once more. They were the worst raids the district had so far experienced, for the Nazis used heavy land mines which did extensive damage. Fires blazed and street after street was shattered. If this were to continue we wondered whether anything would be left of West Ham. But the Luftwaffe had struck its last blow for the time being. The capital stood unconquered and the spirit of its citizens unbroken. The battle for London had been won.

As far as the life of the church was concerned, recovery began almost at once. Normal services and activities had been severely restricted throughout the winter of the blitz and at first it appeared that the church itself would be bound to disintegrate. Yet the nucleus remained and it was a sound one. There was much leeway to be made up. The youth organizations, such as scouts, guides and brigades, had preserved their identity through the service they had rendered throughout the winter, but their numbers had been greatly reduced, and with the quieter days and nights they were able to plan their programmes once more and recruit new members.

The service for women had never stopped. On the first Monday afternoon of the blitz a small group of not more than twenty met in the church and joined my mother in prayers for the stricken homes and the great family of wives and mothers they represented. As they prayed, the sirens sounded and the bombers came over again; so the service was continued in the passages where there was better protection from blast. Monday after Monday they met, a few more joining them each week until the 100 and then the 200 marks were passed. By the spring of 1941 the attendance was still very small in comparison with what it had been, but between 300 and 400 women were gathering for that remarkable service. All through the war the numbers steadily increased until at the end of hostilities the church was in sight of being crowded again on Monday afternoons.

My brother, Hugh, was just finishing his course at Balliol. He was destined for the foreign service, but he was persuaded to forego this, at least for the time being, and come to West Ham to take charge of the Children's Church. He had unusual gifts for work among children and he developed an imaginative ministry among them as 'Children's Padre'. But his is another story of pioneering in the field of education, only the beginnings of which will be told in the next chapter. But so it happened that the two brothers were to serve side by side under their father for the last year of his ministry.

The end, when it came, was totally unexpected. My father had been feeling the strain of the war years and had occasionally complained of pain across his chest. This had always been attributed to indigestion and no one had any idea that anything was seriously the matter. The first week in November 1943 was the last in his life and it was a very full one. Overshadowing these days was the serious illness of his church secretary, Robert Raffan, an Irishman who was deeply devoted to my father and with whom he shared a mutual trust and affection. On Sunday November 7th, after presiding at the lunch table in the Settlement, he set out by car to visit Raffan and take him an air mattress. As his secretary lay there unconscious, apparently unaware that his friend and minister was by his side, who could have guessed that the man so ill in bed was to survive the other who seemed to be so well?

After talking with Raffan's family, my father returned just in time to preside at the communion service on that memorable Remembrance Sunday. It was the custom for two of his junior colleagues to assist him, one on either side. My brother and I were to have that privilege that night. With his deacons ranged behind him, he broke the Bread of Life to his people and shared with them the Cup of Blessing. The congregation left the church just before the air raid sirens sounded their warning. My father and mother hurried back to the house which had been converted from the home for old men to serve as the manse. I went to see them just as usual and we talked of all that had been happening during the last few hours. After I had left them to return to my room at the Settlement House, they went to bed; but my father awoke in the early hours of the morning saying that he was finding it difficult to breathe. Not an hour had passed before my mother was aware that he was suddenly worse and in a few minutes he had gone.

His people could hardly believe it. Only a few hours before he had administered communion to them. A wave of sympathy and sorrow was felt throughout the neighbourhood. But he had died in harness as he would have wished. For him there was no retirement in the service of his Lord.

The funeral took place in the church on the following Thursday conducted by Dr M. E. Aubrey, the General Secretary of the Baptist Union, and by the Bishop of Barking. Among the great congregation that thronged the church were representatives of the civic authorities as well as former colleagues and friends. Father Andrew and the priests and brothers from the Society of the Divine Compassion, the Anglo-Catholic community who were our nearest neighbours, were ranged alongside members of the Free Churches, typifying the catholicity of my father's life and work. But his own people were the chief mourners.

So ended a chapter in the life of the Mission: no, more than a chapter, a volume. The mantle had passed from father to son and I was faced with the responsibility of planning for the future and adapting the Mission to the entirely new conditions that were to face everybody after the war.

Chapter Five

FACING THE FUTURE

THE DEATH OF MY FATHER made the provision of an adequate solution for safeguarding the future an urgent requirement. It was a simple enough matter to devise a trust deed covering all the property, but the problem lay in deciding who was to be the controlling authority. Hitherto my father and mother had acted jointly in this capacity. Who was to take their place?

This was a particularly difficult question in that the West Ham Central Mission was a Baptist church. This meant that there was no central agency which could assume the oversight; for, under Baptist polity, each local congregation is a self-governing, independent body. Strictly speaking, therefore, the local church, acting through its elected deacons, should have been the executive authority. But the Mission was clearly more than a local church. It belonged to a much wider constituency and depended to a considerable extent on the voluntary contributions of large numbers of people all over the world. The building had been erected through the generosity of many friends whose gifts were commemorated in stones around the church. Surely it would not be right for the local people to have the sole voice in the conduct of affairs. Moreover, an enterprise on so large a scale demanded the best advice and experience that could be brought to bear upon its policies.

For these reasons my father and mother were quite convinced that it would be both wrong and impracticable for the control to be vested in the local community. On the other hand they were not at all convinced about the advisability of setting up an independent council composed of men and women who had no direct connection with West Ham. This was not a charitable institution; it was a church; and the principle that in all its activities the Mission was the expression of the church could not be compromised.

A former lawyer had recently joined the ministerial staff and he took over the responsibility of drafting a trust deed that met the requirements. Denis Lant had spent weekends at the Mission before the war assisting with the large scout group and had decided to be ordained so that he could give his full time to the ministry at West Ham. He drew up the provisions for a Church Council to be established which would consist of the board of deacons of the local church enlarged and strengthened for purposes of major policy by those who represented the wider interests. It was thus possible for an Anglican or a Methodist within the terms of the trust deed to become members of the council and so virtually serve as deacons of a Baptist church. This was a novel experiment in ecumenical co-operation and was agreed in principle with my father in the week before his death.

Original as this was as an expression of the universality of the Christian Church in a local setting – unhappily to be lost sight of many years later when separate trust deeds for the church and Mission were drawn up – it was not the only or most significant development to arise out of the experience of these war years. Reference was made in the last chapter to the visits of Oxford students to West Ham during the twilight war of the summer of 1940 and the much larger number who came subsequently during the blitz and afterwards. My brother, who was an undergraduate at Balliol at the time, had arranged with Dick Milford, then vicar of St Mary's, for me to address a meeting there setting out the need for help in the emergency. The response was immediate, and between twenty and thirty dons and students volunteered to come during the Christmas vacation.

They were from all Christian traditions as well as from secular backgrounds and were profoundly influenced by experiencing the church in action. Long afterwards my brother told me that one of the Roman Catholic students who was intending to enter a religious order came into the Memorial Church one day, stood for a few minutes in silence and then said, 'I begin to understand now what you mean by "The Real Presence"'.

When the students got back to Oxford they decided that they must explore further the meaning of what they had experienced in West Ham and its significance for their faith and churchmanship; and so they arranged to meet once a week throughout the Hilary or spring term in the Massey room at Balliol to learn more of what each tradition had to contribute to the fullness of the Christian faith. This was no ordinary SCM discussion group, but an attempt to listen to one another and share their experience. Senior members of the university were invited to speak to them about what was essential to their own tradition and to introduce what they had to say by offering a prayer representative of it.

This presented difficulties for Father D'Arcy, the Jesuit Principal of Campion Hall. Vatican II and the openness of Roman Catholics to other Christians still lay in the future. My brother tells me that Father D'Arcy walked round the garden quad at Balliol with him in deep distress about what in conscience he was entitled to do. Finally he said with great hesitation, 'Perhaps I could possibly say the Lord's Prayer'. This he did, and few of those present realized what for him was an enormous step to take.

As part of the exploration of this group, they attended a celebration of the Orthodox liturgy in the chapel of Lady Margaret Hall: the first time this had ever taken place there and it was talked of by those who shared in it for many years afterwards. Looking back, it is difficult to realize now the impact this made on the members of the group, but its significance lies not only in the influence on those who came to the faith for the first time or whose Christian understanding and vision was broadened, but also the experience of what could happen when Christians engaged together across the denominational frontiers in service to those in need: an experience which is being increasingly confirmed as ecumenism has developed and become a reality.

To return to West Ham. The establishment of the church council gave visible expression to the expanding work of the Mission. The influence of this ministry was felt far beyond the bounds of the locality. One medium through which it spread was broadcasting. Reference has already been made to the service relayed from the shelter during the blitz. But in the early months of 1944 the religious department of the BBC under James Welch and Eric Fenn decided to invite a group of well-known broadcasters to collaborate in a series of consecutive Sunday evening sevices over three months designed as a coherent presentation of the Christian gospel. I found myself invited to participate as a very junior member of a team which included such well-known names as C. H. Dodd, James Stewart, F. A. Cockin and John Maud. I was assigned the last three Sundays of the series – on Passion Sunday, Palm Sunday and Easter Day – and the SCM press published all the addresses under the title *Man's Dilemma and God's Answer*. The whole congregation at West Ham realized that this was a great opportunity for corporate Christian witness, and they responded accordingly.

The impact of these services doubtless led to other invitations to broadcast and I found myself gradually drawn into wider spheres of influence. I was appointed a member of the central religious advisory committee of the BBC, and I was asked to be responsible for the second epilogue on television, then in its infancy after the war. I suppose this also led to my becoming involved in Arthur Rank's promotion of religious films. At any rate I was asked to go to Elstree on two occasions: on the first to make an epilogue for showing in the cinemas on Sunday nights: on the second to make a film of a sermon which was subsequently to be illustrated by an artist. Both were strange experiences. The epilogue, based on doing a jigsaw puzzle, was shot in the set of the hairdresser's saloon in Marseilles constructed for the screening of *Odette*, the film in which Anna Neagle played the role of the war-time spy captured by the Nazis. Making the epilogue took a whole day before the producer was satisfied, and I was completely exhausted by the end of it. I realized something of what film stars go through with constant re-takes before every word and every move meet the requirements of the producer.

The second visit to Elstree proved even more daunting. A replica of the pulpit and chancel at West Ham had been built in the studio and I had to try to preach a sermon in front of cameras and in the glare of arc-lights in that highly artificial situation. What became of these two films and how they were ultimately used I do not know, though I have copies of both of them. But making them was an experience I am not likely to forget.

To return to the closing years of the war: its trials and tragedies were always with us. News came of homes bereaved as anxious wives and mothers waited to hear of loved ones in the battle zones. There were over 1000 men and women on our active service roll with whom we corresponded and to whom a parcel was sent at Christmas.

Fortunately the German bombers had neglected the district since the two dreadful nights of May 1941. There had been warnings and air raids, but they had been spasmodic and little damage had been done. At last the long-awaited D-day arrived and, with the landings in Normandy, the end of the war seemed to be in sight. But there were testing and perilous days still ahead for the people of London and the East End in particular. In many ways the experience of the last years of the war were worse than those of the grim winter of 1940–41. The British intelligence service had been aware for some time that the Nazis were preparing new weapons for an attack on the home base, but the people were unprepared for the savagery of the onslaught. West Ham was within the range of both V1 and V2 missiles. Day and night from June 1944 to the very end of hostilities our people never knew where the next flying-bomb or rocket was going to fall. The destruction was widespread and the loss of life considerable.

The emergency measures which had been taken during the earlier raids had to be adapted to the new situation. During the blitz it had been possible to some extent to plan the day's work. Most people took shelter at night and then the day was given to repairing the ravages of the attack. It was now no longer possible to plan even an hour, much less a day, with any certainty. The Mission staff were on call the whole time, ready to go at a moment's notice to the street where the last rocket had fallen. During the summer months when the flying-bombs alone were used, it was possible to get some warning, for you could hear them coming. But when the V2 rockets began to fall there was no means of knowing where they would land. Superficially people carried on much as usual. There was nothing else to do. Services were held as the bombs soared overhead and the weeknight activities continued uninterrupted. Nevertheless, the constant uncertainty and the frequent tragedies were a protracted strain on the nerves.

One typical incident comes vividly to mind. The morning service had just ended. It was the first Sunday of the month and the uniformed organizations, scouts, guides and brigades, were on parade. As the congregation left the church there was a tremendous crash and the doors and windows shook with the blast. A column of smoke was rising above the houses nearby.

Never shall I forget the sight. Boarding a car, I hurried to the scene of the disaster. The church was on the job. Scouts and guides in their uniforms were moving rubble and lifting people from beneath the debris. Our doctor had rushed from her place in church, collecting on her way a small party of first-aiders to assist her with the injured. A girl in her late teens accompanied to hospital the first of the ambulances to be summoned. On one side was someone she knew to be dead, covered in blankets. On the opposite stretcher were two or three people badly hurt. She kept her head, comforting those who were suffering from injuries and shock, and hiding from them the fact that there was a dead body on the stretcher at the end of which she was sitting. As I saw this fine body of young people in action, many of them just boys and girls, I felt proud to be their minister.

The attacks continued to within a few days of the end of the war; for the V2 sites in Holland were not overrun by the allied armies and were among the few remaining strong points to surrender. One of the last rockets to fall in West Ham scored a direct hit on the home of two of our members, killing them instantly. It was, therefore, with great thanksgiving that the whole neighbourhood heard that the final shot in the West had been fired and the Nazi tyranny had been destroyed.

The scenes were reminiscent of those at the end of the First World War. Streets were gaily decorated and every flag and piece of bunting that could be found was pressed into use. Tables were laid in the middle of the roads and mothers baked hundreds of cakes and buns to give the children a celebration 'Peace Tea'. On the afternoon of VE-day I visited street after street, saying grace before tea, watching the children's races and admiring the bonfires that had been prepared to mark the end of hostilities. Wood had been collected from every bombed site, and there were effigies of Hitler ready to be burnt, each street vying with the next in the splendour of its celebrations. That evening a large congregation assembled in the church for a service of heartfelt thanksgiving.

As soon as the war in Europe was over the task of reconstruction began. The district was devastated. Over 14,000 homes had been totally or partially destroyed and practically every other house and public building had been damaged. Overcrowding was worse than it had ever been and the men were soon to return from the forces. In spite of tremendous efforts to repair damaged dwellings and to provide hundreds of prefabricated huts and bungalows the situation was but little improved. At best the housing problem could be prevented from becoming worse. However, the post-war planners made the fatal mistake of trying to solve the problem by high-rise blocks of flats which failed to take into account the need to think first of human relationships and the architecture needed to provide the context for building community. This had previously been focused in the street where neighbours knew each other and provided mutual support in the grim pre-war years and particularly during the more recent heavy raids on Dockland. We are now reaping the whirlwind in urban areas where high-rise blocks of flats, built at great expense, are having to be demolished because they have been so destructive of human community.

Material reconstruction was an urgent matter, but rebuilding the life of the church and the community was even more important if the comradeship which had been experienced during the war was to be preserved and a healthier society was to emerge out of the ruins of the old. The story of these war years had revealed the possibility of the renewal of the church with greater relevance to the needs of the people in this part of London as well as the country at large. Outwardly it had been shaken and disrupted; many of its old forms of expression had gone. But as Bishop Bergraav, the Primate of Norway, remarked to a leading British politician who was showing him the bombed sites of London and predicting the possibility of one nuclear bomb destroying everything that remained, 'If that were to happen, we still know that the city of God remaineth'. That alone was the foundation of hope on which renewal could realistically be grounded and the fears that were to overshadow the post-war years be overcome.

What was to be learnt from the past and what were the new paths to be explored if the Mission was to fulfil its calling in the years ahead? The experience of the kind of community which had come to life during the dark days of war had made a profound impression upon me and I believed the church was meant to show the way for this to become a reality throughout the land. That ultimately led to the publication of *The Mission of the Local Church* by the SCM book club in 1953 in which I tried to develop these ideas. But as a practical expression of what I had in mind I conceived of the possibility of acquiring an estate in the country where people of all ages and facing all types of problems might for a time live together and discover the Christian fellowship as a healing community.

We already had experience of Child Haven and our scoutmaster, Fred Beagles, who had rendered such sterling service during the war, wanted to give up his job in the city and run a home for boys who had got into trouble and with whom nobody thought they could do anything. He had a deep concern for the lad who had been given up by his parents and who was despaired of by the authorities. He had already shown remarkable gifts for handling difficult boys and he was not prepared to give up hope for any of them. We, therefore, set out to find a place where Fred Beagles' dreams could be fulfilled and my ideas of of a church family centre could be realized.

Early in 1946 my colleague Bodey rang me up to say he had seen a wonderful place in the village of Stock near Chelmsford.

'It's not what we're looking for', he said, 'but I think you ought to see it'. And so I had my first sight of Greenwoods.

As soon as I drove through the gates I realized that this was no ordinary house. It was a lovely Essex mansion set in 116 acres of parkland, woods and gardens with stabling, outbuildings and seven cottages – one of them a period piece in which the head gardener lived. Opening out of a large baronial hall there was a spacious drawing room as well as a billiards room, and in the other wing a dining room with a kitchen and servants' quarters. There were sixteen bedrooms and an attic running the whole length of the house which would readily lend itself to conversion to additional bedrooms if required. The house and gardens were in immaculate condition, just as the previous owner had left them before he died.

This was not the property for which we were looking. We were trying to find a Boys Home, a simple house with a few acres of ground surrounding it where we could develop the family centre I had in mind. Sadly I turned away regretting that it was not possible to make use of the beautiful estate I had just seen. But as I reflected upon its potentialities I began to believe that if I could persuade my colleagues to stretch the vision we already had we could embark on something far more ambitious than we had previously conceived. In 1946 there was no market for large estates and I found that Greenwoods could be purchased very cheaply. In the end we bought the whole estate for £18,500 – an absurd sum by today's prices – funding it from the sale of Child Haven and legacies left to the Mission. The Boys Home could be started in one of the seven cottages and expanded later by building somewhere in the extensive grounds. So Greenwoods became ours and its imaginative development by my successors has made it a centre of healing for untold numbers of people.

In 1946 I had planned a holiday to Switzerland with my cousin and an old Balliol friend. Tom Watson, who was then on the staff of Dean Close school, found at the last moment that he was unable to come and my cousin told me that she thought she knew of a girl who would like to take his place. So I arranged to meet her for tea at the Old Millhillians club in Whitehall. Unexpectedly, however, I was called to see the solicitor in Chelmsford to finalize the purchase of Greenwoods, and so I had to cancel the appointment, thus missing the first opportunity I had of meeting Marjory Tait. In the end we met at the barrier to catch the boat train at Victoria station. Within ten days we had fallen in love and I proposed to her in the Lauterbrunnen valley. At first she said it was the mountain air, but I knew it was not.

When we told the news to our families on our return, they were taken completely by surprise. Marjory's father and mother lived in the beautiful Surrey village of Chiddingfold. He was a prominent business man, the chairman of Hamptons in Pall Mall, and he had been awarded the OBE at the end of the war for his service in taking over Olympia for making the camouflage material required for the invasion of Europe. Marjory's mother was a Scot from Bothwell in Glasgow, the daughter of an engineer who was the inventor of the Acme wringer and a former Lord Provost of the city. They welcomed me to their home with great kindness and generosity. Marjory was their only daughter; her brother, an officer in the Scots Guards, had been killed by a sniper in the attack on the Anzio beach-head in 1943.

My mother was at first afraid that I had been captured by a social butterfly, but she quickly learnt that she was wrong. Marjory had been trained for social work at the London School of Economics during the war and then had gained practical experience in the personnel department of GCE in Rugby. Just before we met she had been working at the Time and Talents Settlement in Bermondsey. She was completely without side and totally oblivious of class distinctions. Her sensitivity to and love for people were the abiding characteristics of her life and she was the perfect partner in all that I was later to do.

In the January of 1947 following our engagement I went on an exchange visit to Canada and the United States arranged by the British Council of Churches. This took me to theological colleges in the main, though I also preached in some of the great city churches on the Eastern seaboard. It was my first experience of the New World and, coming from wartime Britain with its rationing and coupons, it was a revelation to encounter the affluence and prosperity of a country which had experienced war only from a distance. Landing at Goose Bay in Labrador, I saw a piece of white bread for the first time for many years, and luxuries which North Americans took for granted contrasted sharply with the austerity

Our wedding, April 9th 1947

of life at home. The tour lasted three months and I sailed back on the Queen Elizabeth at the end of March to be met by Marjory at Southampton. Nine days later we were married at the parish church in Dunsfold by Cecil Crowhurst, the vicar, who was an old friend of Marjory's parents, and Dr M. E. Aubrey gave the address.

A year before, Queen Mary had visited the Mission for the third time: on this occasion to unveil a portrait of my father painted by Frank Salisbury. He knew my father and had met him on several occasions, notably when he offered to paint the portrait of Hilda Swift, the donor of the Hall of Youth and Rest-a-While, the home for old ladies, and one of the most generous benefactors of the Mission. But this time he had to work from memory aided by clips of films and photographs. When the portrait was almost finished, the artist invited my brother and me to go to his studio in Hampstead and see it. When we did so we were at first disappointed: the eyes and mouth were not right and it did not look like my father as we knew him. When we ventured to hint at this, Frank Salisbury said to my brother, 'Describe your father's character'. Hugh responded, 'He's sitting in that chair impatient for you to tell him to get up so that he can tackle something else, but there is a deep peace in his heart.' The artist immediately took up his palette and brush and, standing between us and the canvas, worked for about ten minutes. When he stood aside, there was my father alive and as we knew him, far better than any photograph could show. It was probably one of Frank Salisbury's best portraits and it now hangs outside the library at Regent's Park College in Oxford where my mother wished it to remain after her death.

Queen Mary had agreed to visit the Mission again to see how it had emerged from the ravages of war and at the same time unveil my father's portrait in the Memorial Church. After the ceremony my mother conducted her on a tour of the buildings to inspect the various clubs and organizations. This was to finish with tea in my study at the Settlement. Before leaving the church the Queen had invited Lady Snowden, an old friend who was present, to join us for tea. She was very lame and could not accompany us on the tour of inspection; so she went straight to my study to await our arrival. The plan was that the Queen would sit at the head of the table with my mother on her right while I would sit on her left, but Queen Mary immediately asked Lady Snowden to come and sit beside her between my mother and herself. This left me to carry the conversation and I was unprepared for it. Somehow I managed. Queen Mary was very formidable and I remember her asking me, 'Mr Clifford, what do you make of the young people today?' I don't know how I answered, but I hope I coped without too much gaucheness.

After tea, the Queen turned to her Lady-in-Waiting and said, 'I've brought a present for Mrs Clifford. Let me have it'. On being handed a small parcel, she insisted on my mother opening it. Inside

Queen Mary unveiling my father's portrait
with the artist, Frank Salisbury

was a book with pictures of herself in war-time. Turning the pages, she came to a picture of herself at Badminton with a saw in her hand. 'That's me', she said, 'cutting down a tree!'

One other incident of that visit stands out in my memory. Queen Mary had been received, as is customary, by the Mayor of West Ham. My mother was firmly convinced that this was the limit of civic responsibility and that the Mayor should not play hostess when on the Mission premises. Accordingly, she was not included in the small party for tea. I was conscious that this had not pleased her and that she felt slighted at being left out. As she was leaving the Settlement House following the Queen's departure, I seized the beautiful flowers from a vase in the hall and handed them dripping with water to the Mayor! The lady who had provided the flowers was standing by the door and, after the Mayor had left, exclaimed with horror, 'My flowers! You've given them to that woman!' I doubt whether I mollified the Mayor, but the incident caused a great deal of amusement.

To return to 1947. During my visit to North America my mother had set to work to adapt Greenwoods to its new purposes and my aunt Mary had come out of retirement to help her. This was a task after my mother's heart and while Marjory and I were on our honeymoon she completed preparations for the opening. Queen Elizabeth the Queen Mother, then Queen, agreed to set the seal on this new enterprise by paying a visit to Greenwoods herself. This was a memorable occasion and hundreds of friends and supporters, both old and new, gathered to welcome the royal patron.

This was Marjory's first introduction to a major public function and she was to discover that upon these occasions you have to be prepared for the unexpected. Several weeks beforehand the Lord Lieutenant of the county had come to Greenwoods to discuss plans for the royal visit. It appeared that he had not been responsible for receiving a member of the royal family before and he was naturally anxious that no mistakes should be made. Above everything else he wanted to be assured that adequate provision would be made if at any point Her Majesty wished to retire! He was satisfied when he was told that suitable accommodation would be available at the top of the stairs. My mother would conduct the Queen round the ground floor of the house and then go upstairs, leaving the rest of the party behind, with the exception of the Lady-in-Waiting accompanied by Marjory. On the first flight Marjory was to ask the Lady-in-Waiting whether Her Majesty wished to retire. The Lord Lieutenant expressed himself satisfied with the arrangement. When the moment came, Marjory did as she had been instructed, but, on being asked the question, the Lady-in-Waiting replied, 'I really don't know. You had better ask her yourself'. The young bride

My mother at Greenwoods

managed to cope without undue embarrassment and all was well.

After inspecting the house the Queen walked through the garden to a marquee for the dedication service. As she left she stood by the balustrade bordering the park where 500 young people were in camp. They were all concealed behind a rise in the ground. At a given signal from the scoutmaster they rushed cheering from their place of concealment towards the balustrade. The Queen was obviously delighted and this was clearly the highlight of the day.

For my mother it was a triumphant occasion. Early in the war she had received the OBE from the King for her service to women and children in West Ham. Now, on this memorable summer's afternoon her life's work was crowned by the visit of the Queen to Greenwoods.

Chapter Six

BUILDING BRIDGES

THE INAUGURATION of the Church Council and the opening of
Greenwoods marked the beginning of a new phase in the life of
the Mission. Child Haven had been sold and a wing of the new
house had been adapted for the care of sick children and mothers
and babies to continue the work that had been done at Shenfield.
Muriel Forrest, who had joined the staff as a secretary in the early
nineteen-twenties, took charge of the new enterprise and
developed it with great efficiency and imagination. She was later to
assume responsibility for the Marnham House Settlement when a
warden was finally appointed for Greenwoods. She remained at
West Ham until her retirement, but then stayed on in a flat nearby
for another twenty-three years, helping and advising my
successors until her death at nearly ninety years of age, still active
to the last after a lifetime of service to the Mission. Hers was a
remarkable record.

Fred Beagles, the scoutmaster, gave up his job in the city and
took over one of the cottages where he began the work of the Boys'
Home. The plan was to build on the adjoining site and we appealed
to the United Kingdom Trust to help us. The chairman, Sir John
Wolfendon, came to Greenwoods with two of his fellow trustees
and saw the possibilities of what we had in mind. As a result the
Trust agreed to meet the whole cost and Fred's dream was fulfilled.
Orchard House, accommodating twenty boys, was built and
opened with high hopes and great rejoicing.

The story of what followed is one of remarkable achievement.
Fred was determined never to give up a boy as hopeless and his
great physique and commanding personality won the trust of those

whom others had decided were beyond redemption. On one occasion a particularly difficult boy ran away and was caught by the police after breaking into a house and stealing a number of valuables. But the police could not discover where he had hidden the loot. When Fred Beagles arrived at the station, he was told what had happened and the culprit was produced. 'Leave him to me', said Fred. 'I'll find out where he has hidden the stuff.' Some minutes later he came back to the officer in charge with a broad smile and said, 'I know where he's hidden it; it's in your police station!' The loot was recovered and the culprit returned to Orchard House from where he went on to make good in a steady job that Fred had found for him. I have no record of the number of boys who were placed in his care, but it must have been considerable, and up to the time of his retirement he was to see many to whom he had given a new start in life coming back to Orchard House to tell him about their jobs, their marriages and their families.

Another development of potentially the widest significance took place during these immediate post-war years. Ecumenism is a word that is commonly used to describe inter-church relations, and the importance of this had come to be seen during the blitz and its aftermath, highlighted in the visits of the Oxford students to which I have already referred. But the Greek word *oikumene*, from which the English is derived, has a much wider meaning; it refers to the whole inhabited world. In Christian terms this applies to the whole creation and particularly to the relationships of people across the national barriers within the entire human family. The Church betrays its mission when it becomes an ecclesiastical ghetto.

My brother's major interest at Oxford lay in international affairs and by his own inclination he was destined, as I have said, for the foreign service. When he was persuaded to join the Mission staff during the war as 'Children's Padre', he brought to bear his unusual gifts and wider interests on the work he was called upon to do. Coming to West Ham, he found that there were many boys and girls who could not be incorporated into one of the uniformed youth organizations, such as scouts, guides and brigades, partly because there was not room for all of them and partly because many had no inclination in this direction. On the other hand, the ordinary type of youth club was not sufficiently demanding and simply to organize games provided no real incentive. This is the problem all youth club leaders have to face: the programme is the constant headache. Was it possible to devise a new type of club which would challenge boys and girls to look beyond the narrow confines of their restricted environment, scarred by the ravages of war, and catch the vision of a kingdom which transcended national frontiers: the kingdom of God which Jesus came to proclaim? This was ecumenism in the deepest sense of the word.

Through the goodwill and co-operation of members of the Norwegian government, then in London, the first international service club was formed at the Children's Church, the purpose of which was to serve the boys and girls of Norway in the name of Christ. The club motto was 'Christus Victor' based on the verse in the letter to the Ephesians: 'He hath broken down the middle wall of partition between us'. Each meeting ended with the members forming a letter V for the closing prayer, the apex being left empty, signifying that the victorious and risen Christ was there and at the head of every V.

The activities of the clubs were divided into two main parts – handicrafts and badge work. At the carpentry benches all kinds of articles from toys to household goods were made, while at other tables needlework, leatherwork and soft toys occupied many busy hands. The members made nothing for themselves and never even asked to take anything back home for their own use. It was all for Norway. Everything was to be sold in aid of some project for the boys and girls of that country. Meanwhile there were badges to be won; to serve others meant that something had to be known about them. In this way the members of the club set to work to learn the language, understand the customs and begin to appreciate the culture of the land of their adoption.

When a boy or girl had qualified for the initial badge an investiture service was held. The first of these services took place in the Norwegian seamen's church at Rotherhithe, conducted by my brother and the Lutheran chaplain. Taking their stand in the formation of the letter V, the members of the club pledged themselves to serve the boys and girls of Norway, with their hands crossed, symbolizing hands across the seas under the cross of Christ. A Norwegian standard was then presented by Dr Devik of the Norwegian Ministry of Church and Education, and he gave to each of those who had passed the necessary tests an enamelled badge bearing the flags of the two countries. The service ended with the singing of the hymn, 'Jesus shall reign'.

The Norwegian club was soon followed by others linked with the Netherlands and Greece, and the whole conception gradually developed. Before long leaders were being trained to take responsibility for sections of their own, instructing the boys and girls under them in craft and badge work. In this way these young internationalists began to educate one another.

When the clubs were well established the first visits overseas after the war were planned. In the summer of 1946 a party left for Norway, the first organized group of British youth to visit that country since liberation. They received a tremendous welcome in Stavanger, Odda, Bergen and the other towns where they stayed. Two years later another group went to Norway again and a party from the Dutch club spent a memorable fortnight with members of the Free Youth Church of Rotterdam, an organization for young people drawn from all over the Netherlands.

The crown of these achievements was an international camp held in the summer of 1949 at Greenwoods. Boys and girls from Norway, Greece and Holland were the guests of club members who had raised the full cost of their entertainment through the work done over the previous years. The ten Greeks were the first young people to visit England from that suffering country since the outbreak of war and they were the successful candidates out of 1200 applicants. Each tent had its flag with the sign of the cross on it, boys and girls of each nation sleeping under the same canvas roof.

This was a highly significant venture. Hands had been stretched across the seas and the minds of many young people had been opened to a world of which they knew practically nothing. It was the Mission's loss when my brother left to experiment further in the educational field, but what he did in West Ham bore abundant fruit in the Resources Centre which he set up in Leicestershire for the schools of the county where teachers could bring classes for a whole day to explore a new approach to learning. An old school building housed unique resources for the study of a cross range of subjects varying from Chaucer, the Tudors, Spain, China, Roman Britain and Greece from ancient to modern times. For a month the latter was sponsored by the classical association at the National Gallery in London for sixth forms from all over the country to come and share in it. But that is another story, though it had its origins in the Children's Church at West Ham.

After the opening of Greenwoods my mother's strength gradually began to fail. She still continued to lead the service for women on Monday afternoons with all her old flair and she remained the titular superintendent of the Mission – a role she had taken over after my father's death. But the weight of responsibility now fell on younger shoulders and a younger generation had to take the lead. Before long cancer was diagnosed and she was finally admitted to hospital for an operation. While she was there I received a letter from Queen Mary's Lady-in-Waiting saying that Her Majesty had commanded her to inquire how my mother was and wished to be kept informed of her progress. At the same time she said that the Queen was sending my mother a shawl. Those who think of Queen Mary as a cold, austere, regal figure may have no idea of the many acts of kindness to other people or of the trouble she took to show that she cared. My mother was but one of those for whom she had this personal concern and it meant so much to those facing illness or some other misfortune.

When she came out of hospital, partially recovered from the operation, my mother was largely confined to rooms in the Settlement House – my father's old study and an adjoining bedroom. She had vacated the manse in the garden to Marjory and me on our marriage. We wanted to have a family, but we found that Marjory could not have children of her own; her fallopian tubes were blocked and an operation did not improve the condition. So we decided to adopt a baby girl. One of the last things my mother did was to come into the service on the Monday afternoon after we had brought Monica Jean home and explain to the great crowd of women present the significance of adoption into the family of God. Her voice was as clear as ever, though perhaps not as powerful as once it was. Two days after Christmas in 1952 she came to the end of the road. The bells of the Memorial Church were pealing the time of the evening service. With one of my colleagues beside me, I stood at the foot of her bed and recited the 'Nunc Dimittis': 'Lord, now let thy servant depart in peace; for mine eyes have seen thy salvation'. Thus ended another chapter in the Mission's story.

With my mother's death, I felt free to look to the future and decide what I ought to do. Ever since my ordination I had never felt that I should spend the rest of my life in West Ham; the family tradition ought to be broken and fresh minds should be given the opportunity to tackle a constantly changing challenge. And so I had come to regard my role as building a bridge from the old to the new. This was the time to move on and hand over to somebody else. Besides, I was mentally and spiritually exhausted; the war years and their aftermath had taken their toll and sixteen years was a long time to exercise a ministry in one place, particularly a ministry as demanding as that at West Ham.

When I told the church officers of my intention, at first they could not accept it, and pressure was brought to bear on me to reconsider my decision. But I knew I was right and at last it became clear to everybody that I would not change my mind. I had given several months notice of my intention and I promised that I would not leave before the end of August. That would allow ample time to find my successor, though it was essential not to have a gap between my departure and the arrival of a new superintendent minister. With a large staff and an extensive programme, the customary interregnum in other churches would have left too much of a hiatus.

So we looked for a potential successor and all the signs seemed to point to Stanley Turl, the minister of High Road Baptist Church, Ilford. It was my unusual privilege to preside over the church meeting which sent him a unanimous invitation, and he agreed to come in the following September, less than a month after I had planned to leave.

Stanley was an old friend whom I knew well. I realized that he would have the strength of character to plough his own furrow and would not be bound by the past. However I determined to put the Atlantic ocean between us if I possibly could so that he would not feel me breathing down his neck or my being available to anyone who wanted to complain about the sweeping of a new broom. In the event, Stanley stayed as Superintendent for twenty-five years until his retirement, and pioneered several new ventures including the erection of fine new buildings to replace those that had become obsolescent after the passage of time. His ministry was a reversion to the pre-war concept of the Mission's social outreach, though adapted to a new and rapidly changing environment. The ecumenical and international dimension of the Mission's vision, the seeds of which had been sown during the war and its aftermath, was lost, but Stanley continued to develop his ministry to the wider Church, subsequently being elected President of the Baptist Union and Moderator of the Free Church Federal Council. But the ecumenical vision was to come to fruition in the federation of the Selly Oak Colleges and my brother's unique Resources Centre at Thurmaston. So on the first Sunday in September 1953 I conducted my last service at West Ham and Marjory and I left for Canada with Monica Jean the following day.

Chapter Seven

CANADA

WHEN I decided that the time had come for me to leave West Ham, my first idea was to take a sabbatical year and, if possible, pursue graduate work in philosophy which I had been compelled to abandon when the call came to join the Mission staff. My choice would have been to go to the United States and preferably to Ann Arbour in Michigan where interesting work was being done in the field of Logical Analysis. However, at the time it was impossible to take any money out of the country and, if I wanted to spend a year on the other side of the Atlantic, it would be necessary for me to get a job over there and at least earn my living expenses.

Fortunately, Dr Ernest Payne, who was then Secretary of the Baptist Union, had been asked to suggest the name of someone who could temporarily take the place of the newly appointed Professor of Homiletics and Pastoral Theology at McMaster University in Southern Ontario, who had been taken ill and could not join the faculty for the time being. Dr Payne suggested my name to the Vice-Chancellor who happened to be in London on a visit. We met at the Reform Club, which I had recently joined, and Dr Gilmour invited me to come to McMaster for the academic year beginning in September.

This met my immediate needs admirably and we set sail from Liverpool on the Empress of England for what I believed was only a temporary appointment, though this was to turn out otherwise. On our arrival in Hamilton we were met at the station by Nath Parker, the Dean of Theology, and taken to the Vice-Chancellor's house on the campus of the university where we were generously entertained for a fortnight until we had settled in and rented a temporary apartment.

We were also helped to feel at home by the welcome given us by the members of the Divinity Faculty amongst whom was an old friend in Russell Aldwinckle who had been a fellow-student at Regent's Park before the war. He had succeeded Dr Robert McCracken as professor of theology in 1947 when the latter had been called to be minister of the famous church on Riverside Drive, New York. He and his wife, Muriel, have continued to be close friends all our lives and it was my privilege to participate in the memorial service in his old church in Coventry in 1992 after he had died in hospital in Hamilton following a distinguished contribution not only to McMaster, but to theological studies in Canada and far beyond.

McMaster University was founded in the nineteenth century by a senator of that name for the training of Canadian Baptist ministers and to provide a liberal education for Baptist young people. For many years it was located in the city of Toronto but in the early nineteen-thirties the decision had been taken to move to a splendid site on the edge of the ravine at the end of Lake Ontario within the boundaries of the city of Hamilton. One of the reasons behind the move was to establish a university in the Niagara peninsula where there was a large population which did not enjoy this facility. By the time I arrived, there were over 1000 students on the campus and a faculty of just over 100.

By contemporary standards the university was a small one and it was possible to hold faculty meetings for the whole staff in a large room in the tower of University Hall, one of the two main buildings originally erected on the site. However, the university of 1953 was to be dwarfed over the next two decades by its expansion to an enrolment of 15,000 students, an extensive graduate programme and the rapid construction of new buildings, climaxed by the establishment of the most modern medical school and

University Hall, McMaster University

teaching hospital in North America.

In 1953 there were already signs of the expansion that was about to take place. The university was still under the control of a board of governors appointed by and responsible to the Baptist Convention of Ontario and Quebec, but it was obvious that this could not continue much longer; no religious denomination could sustain the cost of a modern university, particularly on the scientific side; and McMaster had already established a reputation for being in the forefront of scientific research. The first nuclear reactor for research purposes in any university throughout the Commonwealth had been built on the campus at the instigation of Dr Harry Thode, the Principal of Hamilton College, which housed the science departments in the second of the two main buildings constituting the centre of the university.

But expansion lay in the future even if it were to take us by surprise by its scale and rapidity. For the first year or two I was there the faculty, firmly presided over by George Gilmour, was small enough for everyone to know one another and it was a harmonious academic community. The theological faculty was regarded as the senior one and the Christian commitment of most of the members of other departments gave a distinctive character to the whole place.

Among them were some scholars with established reputations, one or two of whom had begun their academic careers in Toronto while McMaster was still located there. George Gilmour was widely regarded as being in the forefront of Canadian higher education. He had a brilliant mind, great charm and a ready wit. You could always anticipate some *bon mot* on any occasion, as at one convocation when I remember him saying, 'We have to observe protocol at these functions, but we may make mistakes. People who matter don't mind and people who mind don't matter!' He was the architect of all the expansion in the fifties. I have already mentioned Harry Thode, but there was also Togo Salmon, an outstanding classical scholar.

Some of the retired professors who were still around the place and frequent visitors to the campus made a lasting impression on me as a newcomer. The first of these was Harold Stewart, the former Dean of Theology, who virtually adopted himself as grandfather to our children. Isobel, his wife, was the sister of the former Lieutenant-Governor of Ontario who had been instrumental in bringing McMaster from Toronto to Hamilton.

Then there was Chester New, the emeritus professor of history and the author of the life of Lord Durham. Chester was the epitome of the absent-minded professor and, although the legends which gather around such characters are often apocryphal, I can vouch for the authenticity of the many stories told about him. It was the custom to hold a brief service every morning in Convocation Hall during the main interval between lectures. This was generally led by different members of the faculty and consisted of a hymn, followed by a reading from a lectionary and prayers. One day it was Chester New's turn and the prescribed passage was the parable of the prodigal son. Reading from the Authorized Version, he came to the point where the younger son was reduced to filling his belly with the swine's food. Chester read on as follows: 'And he fain would have filled his ...' – there was a pause – 'I've never seen that word there before; it must be a misprint'; and he went on reading, blithely unconscious of the stir he had caused. On leaving the hall together, George Gilmour remarked to the Dean of Theology, 'That was the most umbilical chapel service I have ever attended!'

On another occasion, Chester, who was a keen supporter of all the university sports, was preparing to accompany his wife to a swimming gala. He arrived downstairs in full evening dress with a white tie. When Mrs New saw him, she told him that he could not possibly go to a swimming gala dressed like that, and he had better go back to the bedroom and change into something more suitable, while she waited in the car outside.

After more than a quarter of an hour had passed without any sign of him, Mrs New went to look for him, fearing that he might have been taken ill. She found that he had taken off his clothes, put on his pyjamas and had got into bed! They had just moved house. No wonder when Mrs New heard that the students had organized a sweepstake about the date on which Chester would go back to his old house and try to get into it, she asked whether she might buy two tickets!

Another colourful character was Harris McNeill. He was the emeritus professor of the New Testament and was well into his eighties when I arrived at McMaster. He had recently been knocked down by a car and had broken his leg; nobody thought that he would ever be able to walk again. But he recovered and went on to live a vigorous life until he reached the age of a hundred. He was inveterately curious and with a refreshingly open mind pursued questions related to his specialized subject right to the end. I remember following him early one morning in the depth of winter on his way to the library when the snow was thick on the ground. There he was, striding along, eager to find out what had recently been written in his field.

On another occasion a party had been arranged for his friends and former students to celebrate his ninetieth birthday. He had been standing for two or three hours greeting his guests when I asked him whether he had not better sit down. 'I may be a little tired', he said with a smile, 'but you've no need to worry'. It may have been later that day that I mischievously asked him whether he had read the latest book published on the 'Honest to God' controversy. 'No', he replied with some consternation; for he prided himself on always being up to date. 'Well, I *am* surprised,' I said, 'it was published this morning!' He enjoyed the joke at his expense.

A year or two later, when Professor H. D. Lewis, the distinguished philosopher of religion from King's College in London visited McMaster for a series of public lectures, Harris McNeill was in the audience. He rose at question time and, describing an unorthodox approach to Christian belief, he asked whether anyone holding such views could really be called a Christian. Everyone present knew that the old rascal was describing himself, and the visitor fell into a very unfair trap. The last picture I saw of Harris McNeill was on his hundredth birthday being shown round the new medical school, curious to the very end to learn what was being done at the university. Such characters as Harris McNeill and Chester New added spice to life and helped to make McMaster the lively and fascinating place it was.

I was not entirely strange to the university when we arrived in 1953. I had visited McMaster for a week during my tour in North

America six years earlier. Harold Stewart was then Dean of Theology and my assignment had been to address chapel each morning and be available for meeting any students who cared to come and see me. I suppose that it was on the strength of this visit that George Gilmour had the confidence to ask me to step into the breach when the Professor-designate of Pastoral Theology was taken ill. At any rate it soon became clear that the poor man was sick unto death and would never be able to take up his appointment. So it came about that I was asked to stay on and become a permanent member of the faculty.

This presented Marjory and me with a dilemma. We had not intended to come to Canada for more than a break of a few months and I had never contemplated the possibility of my future work lying outside the United Kingdom. Moreover, Marjory was an only child of aging parents and, in fairness to them, we did not think we could make our home overseas. However, there was no obvious opening for me back in England and so I agreed to stay on provided it was understood that it would be possible for us to travel home to Surrey for the long summer vacations and that this was to be only on a year to year basis. George Gilmour generously agreed, and so we made our plans. We were not to know that one year was to be extended to twelve and by that time, just as we had come to the conclusion that we were to spend the rest of our days in Canada, we would unexpectedly be asked to come back to the British Isles.

The next six years in Canada were very happy ones, teaching pastoral theology and preaching in churches throughout Southern Ontario. That enabled me to get a picture of North American religious life which was in marked contrast to Britain where congregations were small and membership declining. It came as something of a cultural shock to find crowded churches in many places and attendance regarded as evidence of social respectability. In some small communities, not to be seen in church on Sunday mornings would be enough to jeopardize anyone's professional or social standing. The United Church, a union of Congregationalists, Methodists and Presbyterians was, with the Roman Catholics, the largest and most influential in most places. A typical example was the little town of Dundas, about two miles from the outskirts of Hamilton. There were as many as six or seven churches in the town, all well attended and strongly supported. The total population was only just over 10,000 at the time and yet, when I was invited soon after my arrival in Hamilton to preach on Easter Sunday morning at the United Church, I was told that I would need to take two identical services to accommodate the congregation. The church was a large one, seating at least 600 people, but it was crowded for the first service and nearly full for the second with a separate choir of thirty or forty voices for both of them. This sort of pattern was not repeated in the big cities where secularism had already begun to bite hard, but the congregations were still large by British standards. It can be argued that the social respectability attached to religious observance is never a healthy thing, but at any rate Christian influence was, and probably still is, far more pervasive in North America than in Britain.

Besides my teaching and preaching duties I had plenty of time for study and I was able to write a book for the Carey–Kingsgate Press in London on *The Pastoral Calling*, which was later printed by the Channel Press in Great Neck, New York. As agreed, we returned to England in the summers and managed to acquire a house in Grayswood near Haslemere which we were able to let while we were away in Canada, but which served as a base when we came home to see Marjory's parents.

Then in the summer of 1958 I received a letter from George Gilmour inviting me to become the first Dean of Men in the university and to transfer from the Divinity College to the Faculty of Arts and Science to set up a department of religious studies. This was a totally unexpected approach and was in part explained by the expansion of the university over the preceding six years and the decision to transfer responsibility from the Baptist Convention to an independent Board of Governors who could receive funding from the Ontario Government. In recognition of the contribution that Baptists had made to McMaster, a site in the middle of the campus was made available for building a new Divinity College and a generous endowment was added to cover the cost and provide the means for its maintenance. As George Gilmour said, he now knew the meaning of the hymn, 'Go, labour on, spend ...'. He had negotiated the transfer with consummate skill and the minimum of opposition.

The office of Dean of Men is peculiar to North America and virtually covers everything that does not fall within the province of the academic deans. I, therefore, found myself responsible for university discipline, halls of residence, the student union and relations between the administration and the student body. All this I shared with the Dean of Women, an office that had been in existence for several years.

The expansion in student numbers that was now envisaged meant that we had to plan new halls of residence to add to Wallingford and Edwards Halls which had been built when McMaster first moved to Hamilton. Also a proper students' union building was going to be required. Accordingly, George Gilmour sent me on a tour of North American and European universities to see what was being done elsewhere. On my itinerary were the universities of Manchester, Leeds, Nottingham and Sussex. At the latter I stayed the night with John Fulton at his house in Brighton. The staff then consisted only of himself and a secretary with a desk in the corner of the great hall of the main house, and a registrar in an adjoining room with plans laid out which I was able to study. It seems hardly possible that this was all there was of the University of Sussex just over thirty years ago and is indicative of the rapid expansion which reflected that taking place in Canada and the

United States at the same time.

The visit to Manchester was memorable for the opportunity it gave me to stay the night with Professor H. H. Rowley, the Old Testament scholar. One of my colleagues had asked me to find out how Rowley managed to see, let alone read, all the references he quoted in footnotes. He explained that the answer lay in the house where I was being entertained. He had two large studies, one upstairs for his linguistic work and the other down below for his historical research. Each room was lined from floor to ceiling with bookshelves, and volumes for which space could not be found there overflowed into the passages outside. Never have I seen so many books in one house. In addition, Rowley explained that he subscribed to over forty journals and so could lay his hands on almost anything he wanted to know.

Then he told me the most extraordinary story I have ever heard about a photographic memory. He said that about a year before a young Jewish scholar had been appointed to his department and that he had invited him to tea at the house. When he discovered that his guest was so strictly orthodox that he did not feel comfortable eating in the home of a Gentile, Rowley said that in future they would meet socially on university premises. Then some time later the young man asked him if he might borrow a certain book. 'Certainly, if I have it', he replied. 'Well unless you have lent it to someone it is on the fourth shelf facing the door of your upstairs study and the eighth book along'. Rowley said he could not possibly understand how anyone could describe where one of his books was some months after visiting his house, but was told that on that occasion the young Jew had photographed in his mind every book in the house and the exact place of each of them. Rowley said that he simply did not believe it, but that he had been able to check the accuracy of the claim several days before my visit. He had wanted to refer a research student to a three-volume work in Swedish, but he could not remember the title or the name of the author. He thought he would ask his young colleague help him to find it. He was told that the work was in two volumes so many places along on a certain shelf in a bay of the university library. Rowley was sure that the other had been wrong in at least one particular: the Swedish work was in three volumes, not two. But when he went to find it, it was in the exact place described, but with the three volumes bound in two! The young man had photographed in his mind the entire library of the University of Manchester.

The incident had nothing to do with the purpose of my visit, but the story was such an extraordinary one that it is the principal memory I have of that summer's wide-ranging exploration. But I learnt a good deal that was of value in planning our own expansion at McMaster. The tour had begun in the United States where I gathered sufficient evidence to warn my colleagues of the danger of embarking on high-rise halls of residence. At the University of Buffalo I was told that a student had committed suicide the week before by throwing himself out of a window on the eleventh floor of a newly constructed high-rise tower block and it had been discovered that nobody knew him in the isolation of such impersonal surroundings.

In Scandinavia I went to see some of the excellent student residences which had recently been built, designed to attract tourists during the vacations. Thus some of them were the equivalent of first-class hotels, the summer profits from which went far to subsidize the costs of students during term time. We managed to learn much from what others were doing and were able to avoid mistakes which otherwise we might have made.

When George Gilmour asked me to become Dean of Men, I think this was the chief role he had in mind for me; setting up a department of religious studies was subservient to it, though in the end the priorities were reversed by subsequent events. I do not believe that at first he envisaged anything more than a continuation of the fresher courses in biblical literature for which he had written a book entitled *The Memoirs Called Gospels* as required reading by every student. His lectures, more than the book, had been a scintillating expression of his agile mind and ready wit, and freshers who at first thought that such a course would be an unnecessary and boring imposition found that they were privileged to listen to an exceptionally outstanding lecturer.

George used to set them an examination at the end of the year and this produced its usual crop of howlers. The first question was invariably a context one and for a particular paper he had set the words of the elder brother in the parable of the prodigal son: 'Thou gavest me no kid that I might make merry with my friends'. One dim-witted student wrote, 'This was said by Elizabeth to Zechariah before the birth of John the Baptist' and added, 'That goes to show they used colloquial expressions even in those days'. When George Gilmour told me about it, I said that the student must have been trying to pull his leg. 'No, he wasn't', replied George. 'The rest of his paper didn't show the intelligence to have done it!'

When I took over the course in 1959, George had already been compelled to give up owing to a failing heart condition from which he was shortly to die – a tragic loss to McMaster and to higher education in Canada. It was a formidable task to try to follow him in his lectures. However, I soon came to the conclusion that it was unrealistic to think that a compulsory course such as he had prescribed could be continued as the university expanded under new auspices. In 1959 Harry Thode took over the presidency and the scientists were in the saddle. It might have been expected that introductory courses in biblical literature would not have found favour under the new regime. Quite the contrary. While the compulsory requirement was inevitably going to be dropped, I was encouraged to think in terms of an open department of religion which might attract students to choose the subject as their special option and at the same time offer introductory courses for those who wished to take them.

The possibility had been discussed within the faculty, and one day Bill Kilbourn, the professor of history, told me that a leading Canadian philosopher had just come to Southern Ontario to take up the headship of the department in the new university of York, but had immediately resigned when he discovered that all the departments would have to work for the first five years under the aegis of the University of Toronto. He had just written a report for the Canada Council on the teaching of philosophy in Canadian universities and had castigated the department of philosophy in Toronto for not having moved out of the nineteenth century. He was not going to serve under their auspices, and others in the United States were already trying to get him to go there. Bill Kilbourn, who knew him, thought there was a possibility that he would be prepared to come and join me at McMaster if I were to approach him.

Thus it came about that George Grant accepted an invitation to come to McMaster and his arrival on the campus was rather like the explosion of a bomb; for he was probably one of the most controversial academics in Canada. He was a former Rhodes scholar at Balliol and a nephew of Vincent Massey, the Governor General. His uncle had been professor of Colonial History at Oxford and he had relatives in the Canadian cabinet and on the opposition front bench. His academic reputation had been established as a writer and broadcaster and he had been made a Fellow of the Royal Society of Canada. He was later to write a highly controversial book entitled *Lament for a Nation* in which he criticized both the major political parties for selling Canada down the river to the United States. It was not surprising, therefore, that his coming to McMaster should be regarded as a great catch and caused a stirring in the dovecotes.

With George Grant as a colleague it was immediately possible to recruit new staff and before very long plan to set up a graduate programme in religion. We were encouraged to do so not only by Harry Thode, but by the Deans of Arts and Science and the Dean of Graduate Studies. Two young scholars were appointed from Union Theological Seminary in New York and Princeton, and students began to be recruited for the honours course and for the introductory courses we organized in conjunction with the department of philosophy. Students who wanted to raise basic questions by what was on offer, and freshers, facing their first encounter with university work were taken aback by George, this gargantuan figure – a sort of cross between G. K. Chesterton and C. S. Lewis – whose unpredictable sallies were a constant source of delight. I recall him opening one series of lectures to astonished freshers by saying, 'There are three things I like doing and am prepared to do at any hour of the day or night. The first is living with my wife; the second is drinking beer; and the third is discussing philosophy and theology!'

Before long we began to think of ways of broadening the entry into the department. Hitherto Roman Catholics had been reluctant to encourage their students to enrol in an open department of religion and Vatican II had hardly taken place, let alone its results put into effect. George and I decided to go and see the Roman Catholic bishop of Niagara and ask him whether he would encourage students to take our courses and whether he would support us in appointing a Roman Catholic scholar to the staff of the department. He was persuaded to agree and this opened the door to the first fully ecumenical department in Canada.

The problem was to find a suitably qualified candidate. I made extensive inquiries throughout the United States and Canada, but no name was forthcoming. I had also consulted Father Anthony Stephenson, SJ of Campion Hall, Oxford, whom I had met and whom I knew had broad ecumenical sympathies. He was a patristic scholar and the only Roman Catholic at the time lecturing in the Oxford School of Theology. In response to my inquiry, he replied that he could think of nobody. Then a week or two later I had another letter saying, 'What about me?' Of course we jumped at the offer.

Tony Stephenson was a delightful person, somewhat eccentric, but a very fine scholar. He lived in the presbytery of the cathedral church of Christ the King and used to cycle up the main road as if he were in Oxford. To Canadians it was a strange sight to see this elderly cleric avoiding the traffic on his bicycle which was a completely unfamiliar form of transport in Hamilton. Everyone was afraid of an accident and it was said that the doctors on the route ought to be warned in advance. But all went well. Tony appeared safely every day, totally unaware of the amusement he was causing.

There was, however, one problem which we had not anticipated. Tony had his eye over his shoulder at his superiors in the Jesuit order and developed what I can only describe as a persecution complex. He imagined he was being watched and that anything he published would be censored. We had thought we were appointing an established Roman Catholic and that was essential to our plans. Instead we found ourselves having to maintain the integrity of the Roman Catholic contribution against someone who was becoming increasingly restive about it. This was subsequently to lead to Father Stephenson leaving the Jesuit order and becoming an Anglican priest, though he finally returned to the Roman Catholic fold and finished his academic career back in England in the theological department of the University of Exeter. Nevertheless, we managed to hold the balance without too much consternation on the part of the Roman Catholic hierarchy and later several distinguished Roman Catholic scholars were added to the strength of the McMaster department.

In this first stage of development we had visits for lectures and seminars from scholars of international distinction. Mention has already been made of Professor H. D. Lewis, but we were also privileged to have as our guests Professor John Smith of Yale and Dr Ian Ramsey, then Nolloth Professor of the Philosophy of Religion at Oxford. He was invited to deliver the Whitley Lectures – an annual event in memory of a former Vice-Chancellor – and he chose as his subject 'Models and Mystery', subsequently published by the Oxford University Press and widely regarded as epitomizing the core of his thinking. We also had a memorable visit from Professor Marcus Barth, the son of Karl Barth. Tony Stephenson had just arrived and we thought we should not miss the opportunity of a dialogue between them. I took the chair and began by inviting Tony to open the discussion. He did so in the following way: 'Mr Chairman, I never dreamt that I should have the privilege of a discussion with so distinguished a son of so distinguished a father. This is a story which will be told to my grandchildren!' When the laughter had subsided, Tony recovered from his confusion and we had a sparkling interchange between the two protagonists.

The department was by now firmly established and our resources were being stretched by the number of students choosing to enrol in our courses. The coming of the first graduate teaching fellows helped to some extent because they could undertake some supervision of the introductory course, but their oversight and direction placed added demands upon our small staff. At any rate we could look back with some satisfaction at what had been achieved and the future was full of promise.

Chapter Eight

OPENING DOORS

B Y THE SUMMER of 1964 I felt that it was time for me to give up the responsibilities of being Dean of Men. I had enjoyed working with the student leaders in the residences and the union building and we had got on admirably together on a basis of mutual trust and friendship; the student rebellions of the sixties had not yet hit the McMaster campus. One of the interesting things we had done was to explore the possibility of the student leaders' taking over responsibility for university discipline. When this was first suggested, I welcomed the idea and set to work with them to devise a scheme to make it possible. This proved more difficult than they had envisaged, the principal problem being to safeguard those who were accused of any offence from being victimized by their peers. The lawyers on the senate insisted that this had to be done.

When the scheme was finally adopted, the disciplinary tribunal was faced with its first case. A lady visitor had parked her car outside University Hall and, on returning, found that someone had placed an obscene and abusive note on the windscreen. She was fully justified in lodging a serious complaint, and the students elected to the disciplinary committee went to work to discover the culprit, only to find themselves up against a brick wall; nobody would co-operate! The result was that a student assembly was convened, and by an overwhelming majority it was resolved that university discipline should revert to the Deans. But it had been a useful, if time-consuming, educational exercise, showing how trust could be sustained in tackling a difficult problem.

But as far as I was concerned, my work as chairman of the department of religion had become increasingly absorbing, and one small incident sparked off my decision. There were ominous signs that rapid expansion was going to cause administrative problems as the benign and imaginative leadership of George Gilmour gave way to more bureaucratic methods of control. Like many other universities McMaster was beginning to be run as a big business and the pattern of Shell Oil seemed increasingly to predominate. The university had a bookshop and this was being enlarged to meet the growing demand. Suddenly, without warning, mirrors were installed to check on possible shoplifting. The students were outraged; they had not been consulted and if they had been, they would have offered to see that the stock was protected and any miscreant brought to book. Neither had I been consulted; my approach would have been to proceed warily and to have secured the co-operation of the student leaders in whatever needed to be done.

This was only a small incident, but it was an indication of the way things were going and I was beginning to feel increasingly uncomfortable in my role. I did not want to be a cog in the administrative machine and I was becoming more and more concerned about maintaining academic standards when the number of students was expanding so rapidly. I believed with George Grant that our department could blaze a trail, particularly as our subject did not have obvious utilitarian value, but challenged students to think about fundamental questions.

Perhaps this is the appropriate point to ride one of my hobby-horses. When I first went up to Oxford, it was not assumed that everybody who wished to embark on a successful career would automatically expect to go to a university. School friends who went into business or some of the professions, like accountancy or the law, entered offices immediately on leaving and secured their qualifications by in-service training. They never thought of the university as a necessary road to advancement. In Canada, as in the United States, I found that university entrance was looked upon as a right provided one could secure the minimum necessary qualifications; and grade thirteen in high schools – the equivalent of our sixth forms – was geared to dragooning boys and girls into securing sufficient marks for them to obtain entrance. This many of them barely did, and went on to flunk out in the first year when they had to begin to tackle serious academic work or just get by with a pass degree. Those who fell into this category were not really interested in advanced learning and simply came to the university for the ride and because it was socially acceptable to do so. In no small measure this accounted for the pressure to multiply the number of places for which provision had to be made.

On the whole entrants were ill prepared for university work. I found that I had to spend the first lecture explaining to those who were just beginning their course what would be expected of them; they would have to think for themselves, and it would not do for them simply to serve back in essays what the lecturer had said. I remember one boy in the front row shaking his head in bewilderment when I said that learning by rote and copying from books were not acceptable. Again there were those who survived the first year after doing no work, simply intending to leave when the summer came, having satisfied their parents and friends that they had at least been to a university and could call themselves alumni. At the end of the year they had to face exams, and I remember invigilating on one occasion when a student handed in his physics paper at the earliest possible moment to comply with the rules. Glancing at the first page I saw at once that he had obviously written nonsense, but on turning it over there was the following note to the examiners: 'Dear Sirs. it will be plain that I have done no work at all in your course, but I want to assure you that it has given me plenty of opportunity for rest and sleep which will prepare me for what I want to do now. I hope there are no hard feelings on your side as there are none on mine.' But he had wasted the time of the university staff as well as his own.

Not all students by any means were like those I have described. Many had come with a serious purpose to get a good degree and were open to discover the rewards of true learning and research. But far too large a proportion should never have come at all. They required opportunities for further training, but the university, if it was to fulfil its proper purpose, was not the place for them.

The problem was further compounded by the growing insistence of employers that they would not take on anyone who had not got a university degree, or at least made it clear that promotion could not be expected without one. For example, the door-to-door salesman who sold brushes told my wife that he was enrolling in evening classes to get an external degree because he could not expect promotion without one. Again, a young man, whose family I had known in England, turned up on my doorstep with the American bride he had just married and all their possessions in an estate car. He was on his way to Toronto to seek a job with the Canadian branch of an international firm of chartered accountants whose representative he had been in Baghdad and he thought that this would qualify him for a Canadian appointment. I had to tell him that, without a degree, advancement in any profession in Canada was problematical; and so he stayed in Hamilton and enrolled as a full-time student in the university.

This proved no loss to him; for he was a highly intelligent person and benefitted from a university course. But that is not the point. Two questions are at stake; the first is whether a university degree is the only proper qualification for responsible jobs; and the second is whether superficial egalitarian ideas about the right of everybody to have identical educational opportunities mean that many young people go to university who are neither interested in nor qualified for it.

I had a particularly striking example of the way in which the purpose of a university course could be misunderstood and the effect this could have on education. The department of religion, like others, offered courses in the evenings for those who wanted to take external degrees by extension. For one of these I set an essay, prescribing a length of about six typed pages to ensure that students would be prevented from rambling unnecessarily. My heart sank when I was handed an essay of nearly thirty closely-typed pages, but by the time I had read two of them I smelt a rat: what had been written was clearly the result of advanced scholarship and I immediately suspected plagiarism. I asked one of my junior colleagues to find out the source and he returned to tell me that the whole text was copied word for word from two books in the library. Accordingly, I wrote to the student and asked him to come and see me in my office. He turned out to be a man in his mid-thirties who, when charged with blatant plagiarism, naively expressed surprise that this was not acceptable, saying that he could not have written anything so good himself! When I asked him what his job was, he told me that he was deputy head of a school in Ontario! The story speaks for itself. With such ideas prevailing, even in the schools, what chance was there of resisting the tendency to turn education into a conveyor belt with the essential purpose of a university lost?

Of course, the case I have just cited may be dismissed as an extreme and wholly untypical one. That is probably so, but the fact that it can be cited at all is food for thought in the context of the contemporary debate about the purpose of education. I have digressed far enough in riding my hobby-horse, but my experience at McMaster alerted me to the dangers of rapid expansion and egalitarian standards which spread from North America to Britain in the post-war years. At any rate, I and my colleagues in the department of religion resolved that only the highest academic standards should be allowed to prevail as far as we were concerned, and that the study of the subject should be made as demanding as possible.

This was why I gave up being Dean of Men and was encouraged to concentrate on the academic work of the department. It gave me the opportunity to devote time to writing and I secured a grant from the Canada Council to pursue research into the way in which those who had been blind and deaf from birth perceived the world around them. This had been stimulated by reading the life of Helen Keller, and the theory of perception had long been a special interest, leading to the publication of articles on sense perception in American and Canadian philosophical journals. With the co-operation of the Royal National Institute for the Blind an interesting and promising programme had been arranged when two totally unexpected approaches from the United Kingdom put everything on ice.

Early in the year I had received a letter from a former fellow student of Oxford days who was Professor of Old Testament and acting President of the Selly Oak Colleges in Birmingham. He wrote to tell me that the President of the Colleges had died while on a lecture tour in the United States and someone I knew in Canada had been suggested as his successor. Could I tell them anything about him and his suitability for such an appointment? I replied commending the person named as warmly as I could and thought no more about it.

Several weeks later I received another letter from Arthur Herbert saying that when he had last written no one had thought of me; would I consider allowing my own name to go forward? I knew nothing of Selly Oak save that it was in some way connected with Cadbury's, the chocolate manufacturers in Bournville, and during my student days I had briefly visited one of the colleges for a short course on religious education. I am afraid that I had not taken this very seriously and had stayed only a few days, though long enough to take in Dame Elizabeth Cadbury's strawberry tea in the grounds of her large house! That was all I remembered about Selly Oak and at first I did not know how to reply. Then within a few days I received an invitation from the University of Durham to apply for a readership in theology made vacant by the appointment of an old Mansfield friend, Dr Alec Whitehouse, to the newly established chair at the University of Kent in Canterbury.

The University of Durham was prepared to pay my fare and all expenses if I were to go for an interview and I thought it would be possible at the same time to go to Selly Oak and find out what lay behind the approach made from there. So arrangements were completed, and I left Marjory and the children (for we had adopted Tim as a brother to Monica Jean in 1956) in Hamilton while I went for this brief and unexpected visit to England.

Before going to Durham, I decided to spy out the land in Birmingham, and so on a bleak February evening I arrived at the old Snow Hill station and made my way by taxi through the pouring rain to Carey Hall, the Baptist and Congregational college for the training of women missionaries, where it had been arranged I should spend the night. I awoke the next morning to look out upon a grey mist enveloping the campus and my heart sank at the dreary contrast it presented to all I had left behind in Canada. But it was good to see Arthur Herbert again and I agreed to meet the appointments committee after I had returned from Durham. Neither of us at that point thought that anything was likely to come of it partly because my thoughts were primarily centred on Durham and I could see nothing in the Selly Oak prospect to attract me and partly because Arthur told me that they had another candidate in mind whom they had called from overseas before my name had been suggested.

In the event the visit to Durham was abortive. I had a very friendly interview but it was soon apparent that I was not the person for whom they were looking; they wanted a specialist in Reformation theology and I was not that; and one of the three candidates who had been short-listed was admirably qualified for the appointment. Before I left, I went to see Alec Whitehouse to tell him about Selly Oak and my reluctance to leave McMaster. After listening to what I had to say, his reaction was, 'I think you ought to consider an invitation to Selly Oak seriously. I hear that they are appointing Leonard Schiff as Principal of the College of the Ascension, and that shows they mean business.' I had never heard of Leonard Schiff and all I knew about the College of the Ascension was what Arthur Herbert had told me: that it was sponsored by the Anglican Society for the Propagation of the Gospel and that it was to be reopened under a new Principal. I was later to discover how wise was the advice I had been given, but my conversation with Alec Whitehouse meant that I returned to Selly Oak with an open mind and ready to look again at the prospect it presented.

Before meeting the committee, I waited in the office of Professor Eric Fenn, then Professor of Theology at Selly Oak. I had known him before when he was assistant director of religious broadcasting at the BBC. He had been largely responsible for the series of war-time programmes in which I had participated and to which I have referred in an earlier chapter. He greeted me warmly and, taking me by the arm, led me upstairs to the room where the interview was to be held. I cannot remember much about it except that those who were present seemed interested in what I had done, but it was made clear that they could not come to any immediate decision as they were already committed to seeing someone else.

So I returned to Canada to tell Marjory that nothing would come of my visit to England and that we must prepare to spend the rest of our days in Canada. We had already built a house which fully met our needs in the village of Ancaster just outside Hamilton and the children were settled in schools. Then a fortnight later a telegram arrived from Selly Oak with an invitation to accept the Presidency of the Colleges and a promise that a letter would follow.

The first thing I did was to consult the Revd Gwenyth Hubble who was at that time an Associate Secretary of the World Council of Churches with responsibility for the New York office concerned with world mission. Before that she had been the highly regarded Principal of Carey Hall and she knew the Selly Oak Colleges intimately. She wrote me a carefully balanced letter setting out the conflicting claims of Selly Oak and McMaster, but at first the bias of her advice seemed to weigh in favour of staying where I was. I only discovered much later that she had been behind the original suggestion that I should be approached, though she was cautious about unduly influencing me. However, as Marjory and I talked over the invitation and prayed for guidance we gradually came to the conclusion that I should accept.

It was a wrench to leave McMaster and the many friends we had made, particularly George Grant with whom I had formed the strongest bonds of comradeship. But we believed the decision was the right one, though we had no idea of the exciting and challenging prospect ahead of us. We managed to secure a place for Monica Jean, later to be called Nicky, at St Mary's Wantage and she went in advance to be ready for the beginning of the summer term. Marjory followed shortly with Tim, then nearly nine years of age, and I stayed on a few days longer before setting sail from New York to Southampton to clear up and dispose of our possessions which we were not taking back to England. Our destination was Chiddingfold where we were able to stay with Marjory's mother until the house on the Selly Oak campus was ready for occupation.

I have been persuaded to end this chapter by quoting what was written on the fly-leaf of a book about Canada which was presented to me by the faculty club before leaving. It was written by Peter Smith, then on the administrative staff of the university and later to become the director of the Centre for the Arts at Dartmouth College, New Hampshire and more recently to hold the same position at Columbia University, New York. Nobody can make a fair or objective appraisal of themselves or properly assess what their gifts are. The only excuse for quoting with much hesitation what Peter wrote is that it is said to represent what others thought at the time and gave me the encouragement I needed to embark on what for me was a wholly uncharted course. This is what he wrote:

'I was thinking how appropriate it is that we should be saying this official farewell to Paul Clifford on St George's Day – the Birthday of Shakespeare, Wordsworth and Rupert Brooke, for no corner of a foreign field was ever more English than where Paul stood. He has joined the ranks of those fortunate people who have found a job worth doing in the place where they really want to do it – and we are bound to congratulate him on this, as well as on the more general grounds of having been appointed to an important post in the academic life of the British churches. But there is no doubt at all that Selly Oak's gain is McMaster's loss, and we cannot help feeling sorry for ourselves. It is not just that we are losing a man who has built up from scratch the Department of Religion to the point where it has become one of the intellectual ornaments of McMaster. Nor is it mainly that in losing him we lose a man who taught a whole generation of student officers here the meaning of the word courtesy. The hardest thing is that, at Paul Clifford's going, we are losing a true university man. He is someone who knows that, whatever comes, a university man's life rests on two foundations – a true love of knowledge, and a real concern for students. Few of us, perhaps, realize the extent to which Paul has always been a man to whom students turned – not only when he was Dean of Men, but at every stage of his career here. These students went to him because they knew not only that he knows what he is talking about but also that he really cared about what they had to say. They discovered what his friends have always known – that he is rich in honesty and compassion – and totally devoid of cynicism and guile. No university can easily spare such a man – McMaster is no exception. And, as if this were not enough, many here besides myself know that we are losing a true friend – a warm, generous, serious, but above all, kindly man. It is because we regret your departure so much, Paul, that the depth of our good wishes is so great. We hope that with Marjory and the children you will find in your work in Birmingham a task to match your talents and all the happiness you deserve. You have stood among the alien corn for twelve years. Now you have a new field to plough, and we wish you well in it.'

As I read these words again I am both humbled and honoured. If it had been my obituary, I could only have been profoundly grateful for its generosity and acknowledged that anything I had been able to do I owed to the abounding grace of God, to the wonderful partnership with Marjory, and to the support and kindness of my friends and colleagues. But at this watershed of my life and career it seemed like confirmation of my decision to go to Selly Oak and a source of encouragement for whatever lay ahead.

Chapter Nine

EARLY DAYS AT SELLY OAK

I WAS NOT DUE to take up my responsibilities as President of the Selly Oak Colleges until the beginning of the academic year in September, but it was suggested that I should begin to make myself acquainted with the campus by spending a few days in each college during what remained of the summer term. This enabled me to start finding my way around what was at first a bewildering complex both in terms of their administration and also of the land on which they were built. On my arrival I was handed a coloured and chequered plan which was meant to show what land belonged to the Bournville Village Trust, what was the freehold property of the federation and what was the freehold of each of the individual colleges. But the plan was complicated by the various leaseholds under which most of the land was held. I used to refer to it as my bible, though it took me some time to fathom it.

In 1965 the colleges were nine in number, eight of which were situated on either side of the Bristol Road on the outskirts of the Bournville village which was originally designed as a garden suburb for the workers in Cadbury's factory. This was four miles from the centre of the city of Birmingham and two miles the other way from Longbridge, the site of the British Motor Works. When later I used to take visitors around the campus through the gardens and playing fields, screened from the main road by trees, I used to feel I was in the midst of the country and, knowing I was within the city limits, I was walking on gold. One of the colleges, Avoncroft, founded by George Cadbury principally for agricultural workers, was some two miles away in Bromsgrove and was related to the rest only peripherally; it was soon to be taken over by the Birmingham City Council for their programme in adult education.

Each college was independent with its own board of governors, principal, staff and student body. Five had been founded in the years leading up to the First World War, and in 1922 Edward Cadbury, then chairman of the chocolate firm, saw the possibility of a federation which would enable them to work together for common purposes. Accordingly, he set up a trust whereby he gave to them corporately land, central buildings and endowments to be administered under a council of which he was the first chairman. The trust deed was so broadly drawn that it made possible the admission of other colleges as time passed. When I arrived the central buildings included an excellent library, the George Cadbury Hall for general and public functions and Central House, providing lecture and seminar rooms as well as offices for the core teaching staff which was at the disposal of all the colleges and added greatly to their resources.

This central staff consisted of Professors of the Old Testament, New Testament, Theology, World Mission and Islam, as well as two lecturers in social studies. Until 1959 the responsibility for co-ordination and administration had rested with a Registrar, but on his retirement it was decided that more initiatives needed to be taken to fulfil the potentiality of the federation which Edward Cadbury had envisaged, and so Dr Thomas Finnegan from Coleraine in Northern Ireland was appointed the first President, charged with the development of the Selly Oak Colleges along new lines. This was the commission I inherited following his untimely death, but he had already sowed the seeds of expansion during his brief term of office and I felt that the ground had been well prepared. I knew that I had to be careful not to overstep the boundaries of the internal affairs of the various colleges where my writ did not run. My responsibility was for the central operation, but I was encouraged to believe that fostering co-operation and

110

taking new initiatives would be warmly welcomed. This proved to be the case, and I could not have had more generous support from my colleagues on the central staff as well as from the principals of the colleges themselves.

The structure of the federation, therefore, was not unlike that of Oxford and Cambridge where independent, self-governing colleges are held together within the university which provides additional common resources. So the last part of the summer term was spent in getting to know the different colleges and their staffs.

The first of these was Woodbrooke, established in 1903 by George Cadbury, the founder of the firm, who gave up his house to the Society of Friends for it to become their international study centre. Ever since, not only Quakers, but many others besides, have looked to Woodbrooke as a source of inspiration. Mahatma Gandhi and Kenyatta were among its distinguished visitors; Enoch Powell studied there under Dr Rendell Harris, working on the latter's collection of Greek papyri which were housed in the central library, and the results of his work were published in a monograph by the Cambridge University Press. As a student, Dr Visser t'Hooft, later the first general secretary and architect of the World Council of Churches, also came to Woodbrooke to study under Rendell Harris and met his wife there. Both he and Enoch Powell. whose careers led in such different directions, were later to tell me how much the college and Rendell Harris in particular had meant to them. When I came to visit other countries in the interests of Selly Oak I was to learn how widespread Woodbrooke's influence had been, not least in establishing study centres elsewhere, notably at Pendle Hills in Pennsylvania.

Three of the other colleges were the foundations of missionary societies: Kingsmead by the Methodists, Carey Hall by the Baptist Missionary Society and the London Missionary Society, and the College of the Ascension by the United Society for the Propagation of the Gospel – all for training women missionaries for the different fields in which they were working. By 1965 both Kingsmead and the College of the Ascension had decided to include men as well as women in their training programmes, and a year later Carey Hall did the same by amalgamating with St Andrew's College, founded in 1946 for men candidates and later for their wives by the Baptists, Congregationalists, Methodists and Presbyterians, and renamed St Andrew's Hall under the new Principal, Stanley Wilton.

Westhill was by far the largest college with over four hundred students and nearly forty members of staff. It had been founded in 1907 to pioneer in the field of Christian education for the British Free Churches, and had become a recognized college of education under the Department of Education and Science and therefore funded by the government. In addition to training teachers, it had a section offering courses leading to the Certificate in Youth or Community Service and another section concentrating on church education mainly for students coming from the developing countries of the Third World. The size of Westhill as well as its responsibility to the Department of Education and Science obviously created problems in relation to the rest of the colleges, the student bodies of which numbered an average of fifty or sixty, and which for the most part were responsible to church organizations.

Overdale was the smallest of the colleges, founded in 1920 for the training of ministers of the Churches of Christ. It was to close in the early nineteen-seventies when there was a union with the United Reformed Church and students in consequence were sent for training to one of their colleges. After I had retired, on the initiative of American members of the Churches of Christ a new college called Springfield was established and affiliated to the federation.

The other two colleges were Fircroft and Avoncroft, designed by George Cadbury the younger to provide a liberal education for one year for men from industry and agriculture respectively – men who had not had the opportunity for further education before and who, it was hoped, would return to their jobs better equipped for leadership on the shop floor or on the farm as the case might be. George Cadbury had been greatly influenced by the Danish Folk High School Movement and to a large extent the two colleges had been modelled on that. As I have already indicated, Avoncroft was only peripherally attached to the Selly Oak federation by 1965, and was soon to be taken over by the Birmingham City Council, but Fircroft remained as a healthy challenge to the rest of the colleges with their explicit religious foundations. Most of the men who came to Fircroft were trade unionists, left-wing and highly motivated. Some of them were rebels against the established order, and to maintain some kind of coherence, let alone discipline, within the college community was no easy task and demanded great skill and patience.

Fircroft was the last college at which I stayed at the end of that introductory term. The warden, Philip Hopkins, was a remarkable man. He was a humanist of complete integrity. Though not a Christian believer, he was sensitive to those who did not share his views; he was open-minded and sought to introduce his students, many of whom came with closed minds, to ideas they had never encountered before. He proved to be one of my most valued colleagues and became a very close friend.

He had told me that he had a student that term who was the only one whom he had been compelled to send down for a fortnight for drunk and disorderly conduct and who was one of the most difficult and rebellious men with whom he had had to deal. There was to be an end of term concert that evening, and this particular student had chosen to perform a sketch in which he was to play the part of Philip interviewing himself, played by another student. In the role of Philip, he listened patiently and reasonably to the other being abusive and completely impossible. I wondered how the sketch was going to end. Suddenly he swept the papers off the table, stood up and burst out, 'Get the hell out of here!' As I left the hall with Philip, I said, 'You'll never have a greater tribute paid to you than that'. I and many others were to learn much from Philip in the years ahead.

So ended my introduction to Selly Oak, and I had a lot to think about as I went away on holiday with Marjory and the children, and tried to prepare for what lay before me in September.

When we returned to Birmingham, we started to settle down in the house built for my predecessor behind the George Cadbury Hall. It was rather like moving into a goldfish bowl; for apart from being in the middle of the campus, much of the exterior was glass and without double glazing we were in danger of heating the garden rather than the house. But it had its compensations; I had only to walk about a hundred yards to my office and, despite the contrast with the home we had left in Canada, Marjory could exercise her gifts as a hostess who loved to be available to people.

The first thing I had to do was to get to know the members of the central staff and listen to their advice. Arthur Herbert and Eric Fenn were old friends and proved to be the wisest of counsellors. But four of us were newcomers, and as I had no hand in any of the appointments, I did not know what to expect. I need have had no fear. Initially I had been concerned that my personal assistant should have been appointed without being given the chance of any prior consultation, but I was to discover how right Arthur Herbert had been.

When I first met Verleigh Cant I realized that she was a very unusual person. She had been secretary to Dr Norman Goodall at the London Missionary Society and had moved with him to Geneva when he became Secretary of the International Missionary Council; together they had been instrumental in bringing negotiations for the fusion of IMC with the World Council of Churches to a successful conclusion. On Dr Goodall's retirement, Verleigh had become secretary to Dr Visser t'Hooft, the general secretary of the WCC, and had taken the minutes of all the major committees. She wanted to spend the last five years of her working life in England, and that was why I was to have the inestimable good fortune of her advice and guidance during my initiation into the Presidency of the colleges. Verleigh was a walking encyclopaedia of the ecumenical movement, and after her retirement she was retained by the World Council of Churches to take minutes of the first consultations with the Vatican and other important meetings. On my way to Geneva on one occasion she said I might look at the draft she had asked me to hand to Dr Lukas Vischer who was responsible for the Vatican consultation. It was between twenty and thirty pages long and she had prepared alternative versions of some of the sentences in order that Dr Vischer would only have to cross out what he did not prefer.

Dr Visser t'Hooft once told me that Verleigh had sat through nine days of central committee meetings and that he did not need to change a word of her draft of the minutes. On my frequent visits to the headquarters of the World Council in Geneva I always felt I was walking in reflected glory. 'How is Verleigh?', I was invariably asked. Her coming to Selly Oak was a bonus I could not possibly have anticipated.

In the absence of a Professor of Mission Dr Norman Goodall had been giving a series of lectures in the summer term of 1965. That gave me the opportunity of getting to know this outstanding figure in the ecumenical movement and he became my guide, philosopher and friend throughout the whole of my time in Selly Oak. Without his support and counsel I should have made many mistakes, and he was an unfailing source of strength in times of difficulty. I was able to pay some tribute to him in the entry I was asked to write for the *National Dictionary of Biography* and a longer article in the Legacy Series of the *International Bulletin of Missionary Research*. But that was much later. Norman Goodall helped me to find my way round the missionary world and was my principal adviser in the developments for a new approach to training in Christian mission which I shall shortly be describing.

The new Professor of Mission who joined the staff with me in September was Canon Douglas Webster, the theologian–missioner of the Church Missionary Society. This was particularly significant in that the Society was planning to transfer its training to Selly Oak and build a new college on the campus. After protracted negotiations this was to come about with the opening of Crowther Hall by the Queen Mother in 1970 under the principalship of Simon Barrington Ward, who was later to become Bishop of Coventry. But the arrival of Douglas Webster undoubtedly created a basis of confidence as well as giving an impetus to the completion of the project. Dr John B. Taylor, a Methodist layman, became lecturer in Islamics at the same time, and so new ventures in training for mission were off to a good start.

But all was not plain sailing by any means. The major missionary societies who sponsored the four colleges at Selly Oak had set up a 'Council for the Centre for Training in Christian Mission', meeting in London to plan the integration of these colleges as hostels within a new institution under a director who would co-ordinate the staff in pioneering a fresh approach to missionary training in the light of changing concepts of what this would involve. This was conceived as being independent of Central House which hitherto had been the focus of co-operation and which I had understood was to be developed by my appointment as President.

Ideas such as 'the mission of God', 'partnership in mission' and 'mission to six continents' were in the air and the executive officers of the missionary societies rightly believed that there had to be radical changes in the old ways of thinking of missionary work. But I quickly discovered that they did not believe that the staff at Selly Oak or its structure were capable of doing this and that they had to take over the direction of the programme themselves. The problem we faced was a lack of trust. The ideas were right, but I was convinced that the way in which they were proposed to be put into effect was fundamentally mistaken. The Council for the Centre was a cumbersome piece of bureaucratic machinery and savoured too much of the kind of imposition which I had seen as a dangerous tendency at McMaster. My colleagues at Selly Oak were clearly opposed to it. Experienced people like Arthur Herbert and Eric Fenn felt that they were being by-passed, and newcomers such as Leonard Schiff were not prepared to see the colleges turned into hostels and the programme of training directed from London.

My task, therefore, was to seek to restore trust and to find a way forward that would fulfil the legitimate aspirations of the missionary executives without fundamentally damaging the collegiate and federal structure of Selly Oak. In this Norman Goodall was a tower of strength and I had the support of all my colleagues. At first the members of the Council for the Centre thought I was being obstructive, and Harry Morton in particular, who was then secretary of the Methodist Missionary Society, took me to task for frustrating the plans they had in mind. Harry was one of the most creative minds in the British churches in the sixties and seventies, and ultimately became the general secretary of the British Council of Churches to which he brought distinctive qualities of leadership. I greatly respected him and shared his vision. But it was some time before we came to see eye to eye. This we did in the end and he was the greatest support to me in reaching the solution at which we finally arrived.

After much protracted discussion in which the executive officers of the missionary societies came to accept that I and my colleagues were only too anxious to bring into effect the ideas which had originally motivated them, the Council for the Centre was abandoned and agreement was reached to incorporate a department of mission within the central structure of the colleges under a dean who would co-ordinate the staff of the four missionary colleges with a strengthened central staff. In this way the independence of the individual colleges would be preserved while their teaching resources would be combined with those the central staff could supply. This arrangement was to work extremely well, and David Lyon, an experienced Church of Scotland missionary from the United Church of North India was appointed as the first dean in September 1967.

My other major preoccupation during this first year was to follow up the contacts which my predecessor Tom Finnegan had made with the missionary societies of Germany and Scandinavia. Gwenyth Hubble, from her perspective within the World Council of Churches, had been concerned that those going to the Third World from predominantly Lutheran countries had had no ecumenical exposure before leaving and therefore were unprepared for working with churches other than their own. The majority also needed to learn English as the common language of the countries to which they were being sent, but by using secular language schools for this purpose European candidates were denied the possibility of participating in the kind of ecumenical training that was being developed in Selly Oak. Gwenyth was, therefore, in the forefront of those who had urged upon Tom Finnegan the need to establish a department for teaching English as a foreign language.

Accordingly, I followed up the correspondence that had been left on my desk, visiting Scandinavia and Germany and meeting the executive officers of the national missionary councils and the various mission boards. I had first of all to persuade them that we were capable of offering courses which were professionally competent and at least comparable in quality to those being provided in the language schools they were using. In the second place, they had to be convinced that Lutheran students would not feel isolated and threatened in a predominantly non-Lutheran environment. This latter concern, which was particularly felt in Norway and Finland, was echoed by our desire to have a genuine

Lutheran presence in Selly Oak to which the rest of the students, in what was to be the department of mission, could be exposed. I, therefore, proposed that we should look to the appointment of a Lutheran lecturer on the central staff funded by the European societies. This took some time to bring about, but the new step in ecumenical co-operation was pioneered two years later when Dr Johannes Aargard, the leading Danish missiologist from Aarhus, with his wife Anna Marie, herself a theologian of international repute, spent the summer term at Selly Oak, both of them lecturing and conducting seminars. But the immediate requirement was to set up a department of English and recruit the necessary staff. We were fortunate in being able to appoint Colin Ramsay, a former CMS missionary in Kenya, who was admirably qualified as a linguistic specialist and who was to head the department with great success for the next twenty-five years.

Training for mission, though at the heart of the Selly Oak enterprise, by no means set the boundaries of the concerns of the colleges. Social studies had for long been part of the central teaching programme and, under my predecessor, a course for fifteen students, resident in the different colleges, for training in Child Care had been started, funded by the Home Office. When I arrived I found that we were being asked to double the numbers, and the expansion of training in social work, particularly in relation to overseas students, was something we could undertake in creative balance with developments in the mission programme. To do this it was necessary to find someone to direct and develop a department of social studies, and again we were fortunate in finding an Anglican layman, Geoffrey Allen, who proved to be an ideal appointment, developing the department in imaginative ways to which I will be making reference later. He took up residence in the following year in the old St Andrew's College which had been closed on amalgamation with Carey Hall. From there he began the developments which were to lead to such fruitful results, and in the end became Vice-President of the colleges in my closing years.

Thus in 1965/6 foundations were laid for all that was to follow. But I had no idea where they were ultimately to lead or of the scope of international and ecumenical co-operation which was to characterize Selly Oak in the years to come. My successors were to reap the benefits as well as the problems.

Chapter Ten

EXPANSION

WHEN EDWARD CADBURY established the federation in 1922, he set up a governing council and a board of trustees representative of all the colleges. When I came to Selly Oak his nephew, Charles Gillett, a director of Cadbury's, was chairman and treasurer, assisted by his brother, Joseph, who was an accountant by profession and who was in charge of the finances of the colleges. Charles was a warm, friendly man who, though playing his cards close to his chest, encouraged me to think in terms of expansion and the fulfilment of the ideas which had motivated the appointment of the first President in 1959.

On his unexpected death in 1968 the question arose about who should succeed him. Following extensive consultations, I was advised that we should look beyond the Cadbury and Birmingham catchment area and try to find someone with an international reputation in the educational field. The name of Sir Robert Birley, the former headmaster of Eton and Charterhouse was suggested. He had been responsible for reorganizing the educational system in the British zone of Germany after the war and had more lately been Professor of Education at the South African University of Witwatersrand. In 1968 he had become Gresham Professor of Logic at the City University in London. When I asked Sir Kenneth Grubb, the chairman of the Church Missionary Society, what he thought of the idea, he characteristically replied, 'He can read and write. I think you should ask him!'

So I went to Lomans, Sir Robert's house in Somerset, to see whether he would consider what I had in mind. He and Lady Birley received me with great kindness and, after I had explained

121

the picture of Selly Oak as I saw it, he agreed to become the new chairman of the Central Council. This gave us just the boost we needed, Sir Robert's reputation ensured the standing of the colleges in public estimation, and I had someone to whom I could turn for advice and help in any difficulty. He had an old boy placed in almost every position of influence, and he once told me that, in approaching an official in the interests of an African who had difficulties about his passport and on being asked whether he was suggesting that the official should break the rules, he had replied, 'Not break them, but bend them!' This was his attitude to bureaucracy and administration. On one occasion I asked him what would happen to the ordering of public life if there were more people like himself. He simply smiled and went blithely on, cutting red tape wherever it got in the way of meeting humanitarian claims.

Sir Robert was a frequent visitor to our home, staying the night whenever there was a meeting or some problem that needed his attention. He loved to meet anyone from South Africa, which was his absorbing concern along with the Selly Oak Colleges during the last decade of his life. Marjory was able to arrange for African students to dine with him when he came to stay, and I remember his pleasure one evening at meeting Didymus Mutasa, who had been imprisoned by Ian Smith in what was then Rhodesia and had subsequently been brought out of the country to study at Fircroft. Didymus was later to return after independence and became the Speaker of the Parliament in Zimbabwe.

Sir Robert was a delightful conversationalist with a fund of stories and wide-ranging interests. Marjory would make sure that there was a decanter of whisky beside his chair and he would talk late into the night on a whole variety of subjects. His interests appeared to be unbounded and he was ready to lecture or give a talk on a subject which nobody had considered before. I recall his delight at finding a book about elephants in the rare bookroom of our library, which he took to bed with him since he was preparing a lecture on the elephant in literature. But it was to his abhorrence of apartheid and his concern for the people of South Africa that he would constantly revert.

There was a story he told more than once to illustrate the cloud-cuckoo-land in which the white South African government was living. While at Witwatersrand, he determined to provide a black school with an adequate library to replace the tattered books they had in a cupboard. He collected the money and the new building was called 'The Robert Birley Library'. When the Minister for Bantu Education came to visit the school he asked the headmaster, 'Why have you named the library after that man? Don't you know that he's a well-known communist? Why didn't you name it after one of your own people?' 'He is one of our own people', said the headmaster. Some months later the same Minister for Bantu Education came back and, seeing Sir Robert's name still above the door, protested, 'I see you've still got that man's name there. Don't you know that in England he's called The Red Dean?' 'I don't believe it', said the headmaster. 'Oh yes, he is,' continued the minister. 'I've seen it in a copy of the *Encyclopaedia Britannica*.' 'If you'll show me a copy of the *Encyclopaedia* identifying Sir Robert with the Red Dean,' responded the headmaster, 'I'll have his name taken down from the library.' Needless to say, no more was heard of it. Sir Robert did more for black South Africans than anyone will ever know. After his memorial service in Eton College chapel, a black South African came up to me and said, 'Why didn't they say what he did for us? He got me out of prison.'

Sir Robert was chairman of the Council until I retired and he was an unfailing friend and support. We could not have done many of the things we did without him. At the time he took over the reins, plans were well advanced for the building of a new Central House on the site of the former St Andrew's College. The expanding number of courses, the enlarged staff and the advent of students from many different countries meant that we had outgrown the old accommodation and, just before he died, Charles Gillett had approved the plans and authorized a fund-raising campaign to meet the cost. The plans also included a scheme to reconstruct the George Cadbury Hall, removing the organ and building a stage house in place of the back premises for the performance of plays, opera and concerts. We also had in mind the conversion of the old Central House, adding to it a swimming pool and squash courts to provide facilities for recreation for the students and staff of all the colleges.

The enlargement of the buildings and the greatly increased budget required the appointment of an administrative officer who could relieve me of much detailed work as well as supervise the developments ahead. But I could hardly have anticipated the good fortune which was to come our way. In response to our advertisement a Methodist couple from Lincolnshire applied for an interview, and that was how John and Joyce Andrew came to Selly Oak. John had been a successful business man and had been appointed the youngest JP in the county when public opinion had become concerned about the preponderance of aging magistrates. After their family had grown up, John and Joyce did not want to continue in business, but do something in the service of the church and community. Accordingly, they had volunteered to assist in the supervision of a Methodist old people's home but, lacking medical qualifications, they were looking for something else to do when they saw our advertisement.

I jumped at the opportunity this presented; we had not been expecting anybody with these gifts and qualifications to apply; but I was only later to discover how much they would have to contribute. When it was known that John had been a magistrate, he was immediately invited to join the Birmingham bench and ultimately became its senior member. This brought him into touch with many people in the city, and this was to prove of considerable value to the colleges. But both he and his wife had administrative gifts which complemented anything I had to offer, and they became my very close friends as well as the support I needed for all that lay ahead.

John became bursar and my administrative assistant. This was particularly important since Verleigh Cant was within a year of retirement and our partnership proved to be ideal as far as I was concerned. On Sir Robert Birley's becoming the chairman of the Council, Joseph Gillett had taken over the treasurership and had begun to spread his wings in imaginative ways which made the developments we were undertaking possible. John and he soon established a relationship of mutual confidence and this tripartite relationship of complete trust enabled us to make progress in implementing the plans we had in mind. One of John's gifts was his ability to secure the co-operation of architect, builders and tradesmen in carrying out the projects we had in hand, and he set to work to prepare for the completion of the new central headquarters and the move from the old Central House. At the same time he found in Jack Hewson, a landscape gardener, someone with whom he could open up and transform the grounds to make them an attractive setting for the new buildings. Joyce became domestic bursar, responsible for the cleaning staff and catering, and the standards of excellence on which both of them insisted provided the material framework within which the expanding educational programme was to develop.

By the end of 1969 the new Central Building was ready for occupation and in January we were able to move into it. The weather was bitterly cold and snow lay on the ground. With my Canadian background I had insisted that the architect should ensure that we had the most up-to-date heating and ventilation system, but within the first two or three days my colleagues on the north side of the building were so cold, in spite of the heating being fully turned on, that they had to sit in their overcoats. I asked the heating engineers to come and see me.

When they arrived, I complained about this unsatisfactory state of affairs and they promised to check the whole building. Returning to my office, the two men said that they had found some of the rooms sub-standard. When I asked what the standard was, they said it was to heat the building up to a maximum of 65 degrees provided the temperature outside did not fall below freezing! I could hardly believe my ears. Expressing my astonishment, I told them that anyone in North America or Scandinavia would burst out laughing if this was suggested as a modern standard of central heating, and that no system would be satisfactory as far as I was concerned unless it heated the building up to a temperature of 70 degrees irrespective of the weather outside. They told me that they had met the standards set out in

Outside the new Central House

their manual, but I replied that I did not care what their manual said; if this was the standard, it was totally unacceptable. They looked at me as if I was being entirely unreasonable, but they promised to see what they could do. Somehow they managed to make the necessary adjustments and we had no further trouble, but it was an example of how engineers and architects can be insensitive to the needs of ordinary customers.

The building of Crowther Hall was completed at the same time as the new Central House and Sir Robert Birley approached Clarence House to see if the Queen Mother would be prepared to come and open them. This she generously agreed to do and the date was fixed for the following May 8th. The sun was shining and it proved to be a lovely day. After the formal opening ceremony in the George Cadbury Hall, I had arranged for a group of students

Being presented to the Queen Mother by Sir Robert Birley
at the opening of Central House in 1970

representing the colleges, courses and continents from which they came to form a semi-circle outside to be presented to the Queen Mother. The accompanying pressmen had told us that we were going to have a visit from 'the real pro' and the Private Secretary had said that all I needed to do was to give her the slightest introduction to each of the students and she would take it from there. In the event I had practically nothing to do. The Queen Mother moved from the gauche senior student from Fircroft to a girl from Madagascar, to another from Brazil, to a probation officer from Amman in Jordan and so on with complete ease, having a relevant word to say to each of them; it was a real *tour de force*.

A happy incident occurred as I was escorting her across the grounds to the new building. Spotting our old gardener who had recently retired after many years service, I asked Her Majesty whether I might present him to her. She stopped and in her charming way congratulated him on all he had done for the colleges. Old Fred Broadbridge was thrilled; to have shaken hands with the Queen Mother and to be congratulated by her was beyond his wildest dreams. He refused to touch anything until he had got home and shaken hands with his wife!

The Queen Mother inspected the new Central House, visiting the language laboratory where classes for overseas students were being held and meeting the members of the central staff and the principals of all the colleges. She then crossed the Bristol Road and visited Crowther Hall which she also declared open. It was a memorable day and we were grateful that everything had gone off so smoothly.

The Queen Mother was to visit Selly Oak on two further occasions. In 1973 it was to see the extension to Central House which had been completed the year before and opened by Archbishop Michael Ramsey, and to open a new wing at Westhill for training teachers of the mentally handicapped. This had originally been envisaged as a new college to be built on the other side of the road on a site between Woodbrooke and Fircroft, but it had become clear that it was far better to integrate this training with that of ordinary teachers in which Westhill specialized. This was not the only new building undertaken at this time. St Andrew's Hall and Kingsmead had both extended their premises to make room for married couples, and we had built a nursery school on land between Kingsmead and Westhill to care for children under school age while their mothers could be free to take a full part in the various courses.

The third visit of the Queen Mother was to open Prospect Hall, a college designed for the physically handicapped. This was the brain-child of Baroness Elliot of Harwood and arose out of the experience of short courses which had been arranged for the physically handicapped and able-bodied to study together subjects which were of interest to all of them. Lady Elliot and those associated with her hoped that these courses could be extended by providing a residential setting equipped for people in wheel chairs and suffering from a variety of disabilities, and they saw the campus of Selly Oak with its teaching and recreational resources as an ideal context for what they had in mind. Unfortunately, while the cost of the building and all its equipment was raised, maintenance was to prove an insuperable problem for a voluntary organization. Local authorities were not prepared to pay the high fees involved and in any case were cutting down on grants of this kind. So the original scheme of courses for the physically handicapped and able-bodied people (PHAB) had to be abandoned and the Birmingham City Authority took over responsibility for funding a rehabilitation centre for the disabled where they could have all the advantages of participating in the life of the campus. Though a modified plan, this was to work well and Prospect Hall has continued to flourish.

While writing of the three visits of the Queen Mother to Selly Oak, it may be the appropriate point to mention another royal occasion which took place just before Christmas in 1974.

One day we were having coffee in the Senior Common Room during the morning break when the young teenager on the telephone switchboard came in with goggling eyes to say that I was wanted by Buckingham Palace. It was the Queen's Private Secretary on the line to ask me whether I would be free on a certain date to accept an invitation to one of the lunches which the Queen and the Duke of Edinburgh were giving to a cross section of different people in public life. I discovered later how this had come about.

In the summer, Dr Lesslie Newbigin, the Bishop of Madras, had returned to this country, and Canon David Paton had written to me to ask whether we could use him at Selly Oak. This was a wonderful offer which we could hardly refuse and so he joined us as lecturer in Christian Mission and Ecumenical Theology for the autumn term. However, before coming, he was invited to preach at Crathie Parish Church while the Queen was in residence at Balmoral. It was customary for preachers to be invited to stay there for the weekend and the Queen asked Lesslie Newbigin what he was going to do. When he told her that he was going to be a lecturer at the Selly Oak Colleges, she turned to her secretary and said, 'I've heard of that place. We must invite its President to one of our lunches.'

That is how it came about that I presented myself at the gates of the Palace on the day appointed. There were eight guests, among whom were Mr Justice Griffiths, David Lean, the film producer, and Wendy Hillier, the actress, who had recently played the part of Queen Mary in the stage play 'Crown Matrimonial'. This was later to lead to an interesting conversation about Queen Mary and the kind of person she was. Wendy Hillier's presence and her recent star part in the film of Agatha Christie's 'Murder on the Orient Express' also provided a natural opening of conversation with the Queen at lunch.

We were taken upstairs by the Private Secretary and the Lady-in-Waiting for drinks before the Queen and the Duke of Edinburgh entered the room to greet us. She was followed by the corgis who sat at her feet throughout the lunch and the whole occasion was delightfully informal.

The staff work was superbly done and those responsible made sure that each of the guests had the same time with the Queen and the Duke of Edinburgh. I was privileged to sit beside the Queen at lunch, during the first part of which she talked about what I had been doing before turning to the judge when the sweet was served. She and the Duke had been thoroughly briefed about all their guests, and this became apparent when coffee and liqueurs were served in the adjoining room and the Duke asked me the meaning of the word 'Homiletics', the subject which I had first taught at McMaster.

I was later to have further confirmation of the Duke of Edinburgh's ability to master a wealth of detailed information when he visited the Reform Club of which I am a member. He spoke at a dinner in the library on the subject of reform and offered to answer questions afterwards however provocative or abrasive they might be. He proceeded for over an hour to field questions on the monarchy, industry, technology, education and other subjects with consummate skill. On the way downstairs afterwards a former ambassador who had met him before in an official capacity said to me, 'I'd no idea that man knew so much'. Whatever problems the younger members of the Royal Family may have had, the older ones to whom I have referred have set a standard of ability, integrity and public service without which this country would have been immeasurably the poorer.

Chapter Eleven

THE ECUMENICAL DIMENSION

THE STORY of the Selly Oak Colleges during the sixties and seventies is not primarily concerned with new buildings and royal occasions, significant as they were. More important was the growth in ecumenism. The basic meaning of the word, as I have already pointed out, has reference to the whole inhabited globe; only secondarily is it applied to ecclesiastical relations; and it is in this first and basic sense that there was a notable expansion in Selly Oak.

Mention has already been made of the establishment of the department for the teaching of English as a foreign language and the extension of the mission department to cater for students from Scandinavia and Germany. But there was also to be a widening scope for social studies under Geoffrey Allen. He was responsible for starting courses for overseas social workers, sponsored by the Ministry for Overseas Development, whereby those with responsibility for a wide range of social welfare in Third World countries could gain some insight into the more specialized social services of the West. He also pioneered a programme for Namibians under the auspices of SWAPO to prepare them for responsibility when their country should gain its independence. Later, courses in Development Studies were made available for field officers in the aid agencies, not only for those based in Britain, but also on the continent of Europe and in North America. In collaboration with the extra-mural department of the University and the British Council of Churches we also set up a programme for black pastors and clergy who had received no formal theological training, and this was later to lead to the establishment and building of a Partnership Centre behind the George Cadbury Hall for deepening relations between black and white churches.

The result of all these developments meant that the colleges increasingly became international communities with British students in a minority. While this was mainly true of the colleges sponsored by the missionary societies in which the largely increased number of child-care students as well as overseas social workers were housed, Westhill too was expanding its own section on religious education for students chiefly recruited from the developing countries. By the end of the sixties over fifty nations were represented on the campus at any one time, and this must have made the Selly Oak Colleges the most international educational institution anywhere in relation to its size. One American visitor who had come to the College of the Ascension for a sabbatical term said to me, 'If I had spent the whole of the summer touring the world, I would never have met it as I have done here'.

The mixed nature of the college communities brought with it its own problems. I recall a meeting of the overseas social workers to review their course as it came to an end and one of the West African students protesting that he had been the victim of racial discrimination at one of the colleges. When asked what he meant and to give an example, he said he had not been served with meat at both the mid-day and evening meals and had to be satisfied with a dish of cabbage, which turned out to have been the familiar English supper of cauliflower cheese. He complained that if he and others had not come from overseas, they would have been fed better and he said that this was a glaring example of racial discrimination. Students from different countries were constantly having to adjust to cultural shock and the staff needed to be both sensitive and understanding.

Attention was given to the international dimension by the appointment of overseas personnel to tutorial posts in the colleges and by strengthening the central core of lecturers in the same way. Edward Cadbury had much earlier endowed two fellowships for Christian leaders from Asia, Africa and Latin America to enable them to spend a year at Selly Oak pursuing their own research and being available to students within the colleges. This was long before the missionary societies in the West had grasped the fact that the younger churches were not only recipients of missionary enterprise, but themselves had just as much to contribute to their parent bodies, and that the only realistic way forward was to think in terms of partnership in mission. This farsightedness on the part of Edward Cadbury was now bearing abundant fruit and over the years ahead the William Paton and Dorothy Cadbury Fellows were to make an outstanding contribution to the mission programme.

Another important step which is traceable to Edward Cadbury was taken in the early nineteen-seventies. He had been concerned for the establishment of theology in the University of Birmingham and a chair was named after him, the first holder of which was H. G. Wood, a notable Quaker scholar on the staff of Woodbrooke. When Douglas Webster resigned from the Professorship of Mission in the Selly Oak Colleges in order to take up a Crown appointment as Canon of St Paul's Cathedral, the question arose of finding a successor and we thought that the time might be ripe to establish a chair of mission in co-operation with the university. Up to that time no such chair had been held in any British university, though on the continent of Europe and in North America the subject had long been recognized as an essential component of every theological faculty and department. With the goodwill and co-operation of Gordon Davies, the Edward Cadbury Professor, we were able to bring this about, and Norman Goodall and I were named as external assessors to the university appointments committee, charged with the responsibility for nominating the first Professor of Mission not only in the University of Birmingham, but in the British Isles. It was part of the arrangement that we would put the income from Edward Cadbury's endowment fund to the cost of maintaining the chair and that the new professor would devote part of his time to lectures and seminars in Selly Oak, while we would have the privilege of nominating up to ten students for graduate work in mission in the university.

This was a considerable step forward in gaining full recognition for the subject being at the heart of academic as well as practical theology, and it was clearly of the greatest importance that someone should be found for this first appointment with an unquestioned international reputation. After a very careful search, Dr Goodall and I nominated Dr Walter Hollenweger, the Swiss authority on Pentecostalism and one who proved to be the ideal choice for the position.

It will be obvious from all I have said thus far that my responsibilities to Selly Oak took me increasingly beyond its bounds into the wider world of the Church at large. On one of my early visits to make contacts with the executive officers of the continental missionary societies, a meeting took place in Hamburg between five or six people including, besides myself, Professor Olav Myklebust of Oslo, Professor Bengt Sundkler of Uppsala and Professor Hans-Werner Gensichen of Heidelberg to explore whether the time had come to establish an International Association for Mission Studies which could link together institutes and professors of mission all over the world. The result of this discussion was the convening of an exploratory conference at Woodbrooke, Selly Oak in 1967 attended by just over sixty professors of mission from the continent of Europe, and we were fortunate in being joined by the doyen of American missiologists, Professor Pearce Beaver.

This was followed by international conferences in different countries approximately every three years: at Oslo, Driebergen, Frankfurt, San Jose, New York, Bangalore, Harare, Rome and Hawaii, by which time the membership had grown to between 500 and 600 with 200 or more from the developing world.

As well as being one of the founding members of IAMS, I was treasurer from Frankfurt to Rome where in 1988 the Association was kind enough to make me an honorary member of the executive committee with Professor Myklebust. This association with the IAMS brought me into regular contact with missiologists all over the world and was of the greatest value for the ecumenical development of Selly Oak.

One of the milestones in ecumenical relations in this country was the Church Leaders Conference held at Selly Oak in 1972 when about 500 leaders from all the Churches of the British Isles gathered for ten days to confer together on the way forward to closer union and co-operation. Anglicans and Romans, as well as representatives of all the other Churches in the British Isles, slept and ate together in the different colleges, and Verleigh Cant and I had the intriguing job of seeing they were suitably mixed! Both archbishops and cardinals were there as well as many of the diocesan bishops of both Churches. The Church of Scotland, the Irish and Welsh Churches and the British Free Churches were represented by their moderators, superintendents and others in key positions. The conference was supposed to be targetted at a mythical Welsh archdeacon, but I doubt whether it produced any tangible results either for such a person or for anyone else. The conference was held in the wake of the breakdown of Anglican–Methodist conversations and some hoped that it would point a way forward to closer relationship between the Churches. Perhaps it ultimately did so and at least it gave encouragement to Presbyterians, Congregationalists and the Churches of Christ to proceed to union in the United Reformed Church. But the conference was much more valuable for what took place outside the formal sessions than for what was done in them. Church leaders met with one another around the dining table and in the bar we organized every night, and they got to know and trust each other in a way that would never have happened in formal meetings; and that probably bore a great deal of fruit in the years to come. Marjory and I were kept busy with numerous sherry and tea parties where we got to know many of the delegates, and this too put Selly Oak on the map for many of those who knew little about it.

Several amusing incidents come to mind in connection with that conference. Unfortunately Sir Robert Birley was in hospital and could not be present to welcome the delegates, and so Dr Norman Goodall, by then Vice-Chairman of the Council, acted in his place. We gave a sherry party on the first evening and I was standing beside John Huxtable, who was later to become the first Moderator of the United Reformed Church, when Norman gave a superbly crafted speech of welcome. After he had stepped down, John turned to me and said, 'Don't you long for that man to split an infinitive!' Norman was a master of elegant style in the use of the English language.

As I was walking over the Bristol Road afterwards with the Roman Catholic Bishop of Minerva, he said to me, 'Well that was very nice. I was afraid I was going to a cocoa party!' We got across the road safely, but it was nothing short of a miracle that many people did. They used the Bristol Road as if they were strolling along a public footpath across a ploughed field and, in spite of all the warnings, the Bishop of Gloucester was knocked down and had to be taken to hospital. Looking after Michael Ramsey was also a problem which Marjory shared with his wife, and it was no easy task; he was quite unpredictable. On one occasion during a plenary session in the George Cadbury Hall when people were asked to identify themselves by name and ecclesiastical allegiance before speaking, a figure rose at the back and to everyone's amusement announced, 'Ramsey, Church of England'. These are a few of the memories among the lasting impressions made by those ten days.

Over these years I became more and more closely involved in

ecumenical affairs. I was a member of the executive committee of the British Council of Churches and chairman of its committee on mission. I was also a member of the small liaison committee concerned with relations between the BCC and representatives of the Roman Catholic hierarchy. When it became clear that the Roman Catholic Church was not going to join the BCC in its old form and that a new approach was going to be necessary, the committee was disbanded to make way for the more official consultations which were to lead to the full participation of Roman Catholics in the new ecumenical instrument which has come into being as the Council of Churches for Britain and Ireland. I was glad to have this opportunity of getting to know Bishop Henderson and Bishop Alan Clarke who were the two Roman Catholic members of this informal committee because I was concerned to find ways of bringing Roman Catholics into the Selly Oak Colleges as I had done in the Department of Religion at McMaster. For two years we had the privilege of the presence at the College of the Ascension of Father Adrian Hastings, the specialist on African affairs, and there were others to join us over the coming years, but the fruits of Vatican II were inevitably going to take time to ripen.

At about this time Marjory began to believe that her spiritual home was in the Roman Catholic Church. She had been brought up as an Anglican, though after she married me she fitted marvellously into the ecumenical setting of West Ham. Canada was more difficult for her, though Selly Oak provided once again an ecumenical context within which she was able to exercise her gifts. It gradually became clear to both of us that her ultimate spiritual fulfilment was to be within the discipline of the Roman Catholic Church. She was prepared for reception by Father Bose, a well-known Jesuit and spiritual director in Birmingham, and it was my privilege with my former West Ham colleague, Denis Lant, who had himself become a Roman Catholic after his retirement, to be one of her two sponsors. I suspect that it was unprecedented for a Baptist minister to sponsor his wife for reception into the Roman Church, but I can only say that it immeasurably enriched our life together and made my task easier in presiding over an ecumenical community like Selly Oak. We experienced in our own home and in the intimacies of marriage what it means to share together the differences of Christian tradition and discover in their tension, but more in their complementarity, the way forward to a more profound unity.

On becoming a Roman Catholic, Marjory found that she had interests of her own to explore. Due to the exigencies of war and the limitations for academic qualification for those who wanted to prepare for social work, she had not embarked on a conventional university course; but at McMaster her natural aptitude and enthusiasm for English literature came to flower and she enrolled in evening classes where she excelled. This stimulated her interest in the poet Dryden, and she set to work on the subject with a keen instinct for research. This ultimately brought her into touch with the leading Dryden scholars and, although she did not live to write the life of the poet as she had planned, she did make contributions to Dryden scholarship and there are three footnote references to her discoveries in Professor James Winn's standard work on the subject.

Marjory also began to be closely involved with the development of the Ecumenical Society of the Blessed Virgin Mary. This was the brain-child of Martin Gillett, a remarkable Roman Catholic layman, who had become convinced that the doctrine of Our Lady, being a major stumbling block in the way Christians understood one another, was a fruitful subject for ecumenical exploration. He made this his consuming passion and was indefatigable in twisting the arms of his own bishops as well as the leaders of the Anglican and Free Churches to give this their serious attention. He had enlisted the support of Cardinal Suenens and through his persistence persuaded theologians of all traditions to write papers and attend conferences at which the subject was discussed in depth. Marjory was his acolyte, driving him to interviews and helping him in a variety of ways.

Martin was a frequent visitor to our house, but he always played fair with me. He understood that I had many other commitments and therefore did not put pressure on me as he did on others; he was content that Marjory should give him her time and support. But I got to know him extremely well and through him met those whom otherwise I would not have had the chance of knowing.

I was also engaged in a number of other ecumenical activities over these years. A somewhat unusual one was to have a hand in bringing together the renewal groups which had been formed in the different Churches but had little to do with one another. The origin of this was an invitation to do something about an organization called 'The Friends of Reunion' in which Nathaniel Micklem, John Huxtable and others had played a part in promoting the cause of Christian unity. This was loosely attached to the British Council of Churches, but many thought it had come to the end of its usefulness in a developing situation. Bob Jeffery, later Dean of Worcester, was then the secretary for mission in the British Council of Churches, and together we set about giving The Friends of Reunion a decent burial in order to put something more effective in its place. This led to convening a meeting of representatives of the Anglican 'Parish and People' and the renewal groups of the Roman Catholic, Methodist and Baptist churches, together with others, to see whether it would not be more creative for them to pool their resources and work together as a sort of ecumenical ginger group. The result was the coming into being of 'One for Christian Renewal', the proto-council of which I was asked to chair. It is now a network of radically minded Christians.

Another venture in which I was involved was the establishment of The Queen's College, Birmingham on an ecumenical basis. Dr John Habgood, later to become Archbishop of York, had been appointed Principal with a view to Queen's becoming the premier Anglican theological college. The buildings had been enlarged and modernized, but the number of students had not justified the considerable expenditure of money involved. John Habgood took one look at the situation and decided that the way forward was to turn Queen's into a fully ecumenical college and he persuaded his governors to appoint four of their number to explore the possibility with him, inviting me to be the non-Anglican member of the group. It was an interesting, though complicated, exercise; to bring the plans to completion an Act of parliament was required. In due course I became one of the governors, a member of the council as well as its appointments committee.

In the latter connection an amusing incident comes to mind after a new Principal had been appointed to succeed John Habgood when he was translated to Durham. A scheme had been established whereby it was possible to offer two fellowships every year to senior men and women in the ministry to enable them to pursue research on a chosen subject free from pastoral duties. It was customary for the Principal and his colleagues to make a short list of three for interview by the committee, but on this occasion they had misread one of the application forms. It appeared that the candidate was a minister of the Church of Scotland who had secured a first-class degree at the University of Edinburgh and wished to spend a sabbatical year studying the subject of liturgy. This seemed unusual for somebody with a Scottish background and we were intrigued to meet him. One of the members of the selection committee was Gordon Davies, the Edward Cadbury Professor in the University, a distinguished scholar and the author of a number of books including more than one on Christian worship. He was sitting opposite me, slightly behind the chair left vacant for the candidate. When he came in, it was immediately apparent that he had not secured a first-class degree, only having briefly attended a first-year course at Edinburgh; but at least we thought we could pursue his interest in liturgical questions. So I asked him what books he had read on the subject. He replied that he could not think of any he had actually read, but he had seen the review of a book on the subject by a man called Davies, though he hadn't thought much of it! Gordon Davies's face was a study which I will not forget. But I pressed on and asked what books on any subject he had read in the past year. He could not give me a single title, and when I asked him what he did with his time, all he could say was that he answered the telephone and wrote some letters. This extraordinary interview left us wondering how such a man could ever have got into the ministry of the Church of Scotland or even survived it. Most of the applicants for fellowships were of high calibre and a good deal of creative research was done over the years. Queen's has made a distinctive contribution to theological education and ecumenical enterprise.

I was also co-opted with Sydney Evans, the Dean of King's College, London as the two non-Methodist members of a commission appointed by the President of Conference to advise on the future rationalization of their theological colleges. It had been an unresolved bone of contention for at least ten years, and in desperation this small commission of six people was charged with making recommendations which Conference was virtually pledged to accept. It was a fascinating exercise in discovering how intelligent people could scrape the bottom of the barrel in order to defend their own pocket-handkerchief of territory. We visited all the colleges in turn and were presented with briefs which sometimes contained extraordinary arguments. Richmond claimed that it should not be closed because it was the nearest Methodist college to the proposed Channel Tunnel! The picture of Frenchmen queuing up at Calais to come to Richmond was so ludicrous that it was difficult to keep a straight face. Again, it was said that it was unthinkable that the college in Bristol should close with all that had been spent on its buildings, particularly because of its strong connections with and use of the University. When asked whether, if the unthinkable were to be recommended, the University would take over the buildings, the reply was that they were too far away to be of any use!

In the end we recommended that, apart from Wesley House, Cambridge, training should be concentrated in Manchester and Queen's, Birmingham and the colleges at Richmond and Bristol closed or turned to some other purpose. We made no proposal that the Hartley Victoria building in Manchester should be retained; it was a huge, ugly edifice which reminded me of Wormwood Scrubs!

Unfortunately, however, after Conference had accepted the report, the Principal of Hartley Victoria, who had told us that he was completely indifferent to the outcome of our inquiry as he was about to retire, became triumphalist and proposed extravagantly expensive plans for reconstructing the Manchester building. This was never our intention. The Baptists had a splendid modern building in Rusholme where it would be possible to embark on ecumenical training similar to that in Birmingham. But the concentration on Hartley Victoria threw everything into confusion. A proposal came before Conference the following year tantamount to insisting that planning should go back to square one, and this had the bizarre result of an equally divided vote with the President having the unenviable responsibility of casting the decisive ballot. This he felt unable to do and the upshot of all the confusion was that the college in Bristol was retained, though the rest of our proposals were put into effect. Their essence was the concentration of ecumenical training in the Northern Baptist College building in Manchester, henceforth known as Luther King House.

These were some of the ecumenical activities in which I was engaged during my time as President of the Selly Oak Colleges. Looking back on this period and indeed on the whole of my time since the momentous events of Vatican II, the story is one of disappointment and yet of remarkable progress. With the exception of the establishment of the United Reformed Church, schemes of structural church union have failed, and those who have invested energy, time and prayer in them have often ended up frustrated. But that is not the whole story by any means.

In 1970 Collins published a book of mine entitled *Now is the Time* in which I was unable to refer to more than four areas of ecumenical experiment in England. The number is now several hundred and growing, and Christians have begun to know and trust one another across the denominational frontiers. This has led to the new ecumenical instruments in which the Black Churches as well as the Roman Catholics are co-operating with a fresh emphasis on local ecumenism. The vision of journeying together as the pilgrim people of God has begun to capture the imagination of a growing number of Christians. At any rate that is how I see it and I count it as a cherished privilege to have been allowed to take part in various ways in this ecumenical pilgrimage.

Chapter Twelve

FRESH HORIZONS

BY THE MID nineteen-seventies I was nearing the age of retirement and, living in a tied house on the campus, we had to begin to look for somewhere to settle when the time came. On a holiday in Cornwall we had met a couple from Northern Ireland who mentioned a hotel at Rockcliffe in Galloway, and that chance remark, a note of which Marjory took in one of the many little books she carried with her, was to lead to friendships and five very happy years in Scotland. But that is to jump ahead. The immediate occasion of travelling north was to visit Marjory's invalid aunt who lived at Troon on the Ayrshire coast. On our way we decided to try to spend the night at Barons Craig hotel in Rockcliffe following the recommendation which Marjory had noted. On arrival I left her in the car while I went to the reception desk to make inquiries, only to find that the rooms were fully booked and to be advised that we should have to go on to the next place and try our luck. Marjory said that she wanted to go and see the hotel for herself and apparently made such an impression on the receptionist that the girl said there was a lady on the front who might put us up for the night, though meals would have to be taken at the hotel.

That was how we came to meet Daphne Crooks. She was the widow of a lawyer who lived in a beautiful house overlooking the Rockcliffe bay and occasionally put up people for the night who were specially recommended by the hotel. She was a delightful extrovert and before we had got into the front door she and Marjory had 'clicked'. This was to lead to many more visits and a close friendship. At any rate we stayed the night in the lap of comfort and so enjoyed ourselves that we asked to come again on our way back to Birmingham. When we came to plan our holiday for the following summer, we immediately thought of Daphne and asked whether we could stay with her for a fortnight and take our meals at the Barons Craig hotel. That was a memorable holiday not least because we found a cottage, our offer for which was accepted on the last day of our stay. We had seen its possibilities and managed to get a young architect from Dumfries to come out that same day to tell us whether our plans could be put into effect.

It was an old 'but and ben' – two rooms with a loft above reached by a ladder, and a somewhat unimaginative extension, forming the stem of a T, providing a kitchen, bathroom and sitting room overlooking an acre of ground bordering on the Solway forest; it faced south to the Solway Firth and on a fine day you could see the mountains of the Lake District in the background. We told the architect we wanted to gut the extension, turning it into a hall-dining room, extending the sitting room at the end to twice its length and building an extension on the back containing a master bedroom *en suite*, a modern kitchen, an adjoining utility room and a second bathroom. He assured us this could be done and promised he would draw the plans overnight, having them ready for us to inspect on our way back to Birmingham the next day.

The suggestion had been made that I should have a term's sabbatical leave from the following January to March to visit South America, a continent to which I had not been before and with which we were establishing links with the Selly Oak Colleges. It was not possible to visit Galloway again in the intervening three months and then we would be abroad until the spring. We, therefore, had to leave the conversion of the cottage entirely to the architect whom we had seen only on that one occasion, but we took the risk and this was completely justified. On our return at Easter the following year, we found the work almost finished and the conversion exactly as we had planned. So we came to own Crinan Cottage, named after the Scottish resort where we had stayed with

Marjory's parents after our engagement. It was a mile and a half from the little town of Dalbeattie, but half a mile from a farm on one side and the nearest house on the other. We thought of it only as a holiday cottage from which we could retire rather than a place where we could live. But this was not to be as I shall be explaining later.

In the meanwhile we set off for Central and South America, leaving the colleges in the capable hands of Frank Weston, the Vice-President. He had succeeded Leonard Schiff as Principal of the College of the Ascension, an office he held with marked success, combining it with the Vice-Presidency, before going to Edinburgh as Principal of the Scottish Episcopal College and later to Oxford as Archdeacon. Our itinerary had been arranged by Dr Miguez Bonino of Argentina, a President of the World Council of Churches and recently William Paton Fellow at Selly Oak. The idea was that I should visit centres of theological education and give some lectures at each of them. However, we began by revisiting my old stumping ground at McMaster, where the department of religion had grown to a staff of almost twenty-five with an extensive graduate programme. It was good to meet old colleagues, though I was made to feel rather ancient by being greeted as the founding father of the department!

From Toronto we flew to Atlantic City to stay at the Overseas Ministries Study Centre, the nearest counterpart to Selly Oak in North America. It was situated at Ventnor, a suburb some two miles along the famous Broadwalk, but it has recently moved to New Haven to be in close proximity to Yale Divinity School. The director is still Dr Gerald Anderson who has become a close friend through the International Association for Mission Studies, the executive committee of which has met at the centre on more than one occasion. At one of these meetings we spent an evening visiting the huge hotels which house the casinos of Atlantic City. This was to see at first hand one of the world's main gambling centres to which addicts come from many parts of the United States. Standing in the bus queue, I got into conversation with a woman who had spent three days and nights at one of the hotels continuously playing the one-arm-bandits. Having lost all the money she had brought with her, she was returning home to collect some more before coming back to resume the senseless addiction. That was on another occasion, but on this visit Marjory and I were able to cement our relationship with Jerry and Joanne Anderson and see something more of what they were doing.

From Ventnor we began the tour through Central and South America which was the main purpose of our journey. Starting in Puerto Rico, we flew to Jamaica, Mexico, Guatemala and Costa Rica, visiting a variety of Protestant centres of theological education from those of the traditional type as in Jamaica to those, like the Presbyterian seminary in Guatemala, which had been forced to adopt a programme of education by extension because of the vast distances involved. Instead of bringing students to a centrally located college, the staff travelled to where they actually lived and worked, bringing them to the centre for short, intensive days of training under the same roof. In this way far more students could be recruited and trained at much cheaper cost.

We also had the opportunity of seeing Roman Catholics at work, often in exposed and dangerous situations. An example of this was in Mexico City where we stayed at one of the complex of theological colleges of several Protestant denominations which work together on a common programme. That was not such an eye-opener as our time with a Dutch Roman Catholic priest, Frans van der Hoff, whom I had met at a previous conference of the International Association for Mission Studies. Frans was working amongst the poor of Mexico City and was under constant surveillance by the police.

My son Tim, accompanied by an old school friend, was following on our tracks. The two boys wanted to keep their distance and not travel under ecclesiastical auspices, but they arranged to meet up with us at certain locations, not least with a view to checking up on their limited financial resources! One of the contact points was Mexico City and there they met Frans van der Hoff. They had never encountered anybody like him, and his commitment to fighting poverty and injustice made a profound impression on them; they were somewhat taken aback by his refusal to let them come with him on one of his visits because he said it was too dangerous. This was not to be their only encounter with Roman Catholic priests in the front line of battle against injustice. Later they were to have the same sort of experience staying at the compound of a Roman Catholic order just outside the airport at Lima in Peru, and they were to meet the danger, faced by many tourists, of being attacked by a gang with machetes in Bolivia, robbed of everything they were carrying and narrowly escaping with their lives. But for all of us the time spent with Frans was the outstanding feature of our visit to Mexico.

The highlight of our tour was our more extended stay in Lima at a Methodist building near the centre of the city. This underlined our awareness that throughout Central and South America everybody was living on the edge of a social and political volcano, and that it was against this background that Christians were having to maintain their witness. We were instructed how to stand under the lintels of the door in the face of an earthquake and we were told not to take any watches or valuables with us when we went out into the streets. The buildings at the centre of the city two blocks away were pock-marked with the signs of a pitched battle between the army and the police only a week or two before.

Our host was Key Yuasa, a Japanese whose father had come to Peru as a missionary of the Holiness Church of which Key was also a minister. He was a man of broad sympathies and an ecumenical outlook. Married to a Lutheran whose mother was a Buddhist and shared their home, he seemed to have come to terms with having a

Buddhist shrine in their living room while maintaining his Christian ministry with deep conviction. We were to have the benefit of his presence at Selly Oak as William Paton Fellow for the following year.

Key had been seconded to the Methodists in Lima for the in-service training of their ministers and he was himself in charge of a Methodist church in the city. I was invited to preach there one Sunday morning and the service was such as I had never experienced before. It began, I think, at 9.30 and lasted all morning, including just about everything – a baptism, the ordination of elders and much else – so that I wondered when I was going to be called upon to preach. The service ended with everybody crowding into the courtyard and singing hymns until about one o'clock, followed by a lunch with all the officers.

Time seemed to count for little anywhere in Latin America. 'Manana' or 'tomorrow' was the watchword: never do today what you can put off to tomorrow. I had already come to realize this before arriving in Lima, but there it was to be unmistakably underlined. I was advertised to give a series of three lectures at a central location in the city, and each was billed to begin at 7.30 pm. Therefore, I turned up in good time, as I would have done in England, only to find nobody at the building. The chairman was the only person to get there by half-past seven and he explained that we would have to wait a while for the audience to assemble. When he thought a sufficient number was there by eight o'clock, he decided to begin and called the meeting to order; but people kept on drifting into the hall for another quarter of an hour or so. I was fully prepared for this relaxed attitude to time by the third lecture, but even then I was somewhat taken aback by the chairman telling me that we would have to wait until 8.15 before beginning because the traffic was so bad in Lima on Friday evenings!

Marjory and I had an unforgettable trip while based at Lima. We flew across the Andes to Cuzco and thence by mountain railway to

Machu Picchu, the fantastic ruins of an Inca settlement on the top of a towering peak. The views were magnificent and the imagination was confounded by trying to conceive how the Incas could have settled in such an inaccessible place. The height was so great and the atmosphere so rarefied that it took us some time to recover from headaches and nausea, but it was an experience we would not have missed. Machu Picchu must be one of the wonders of the world.

Our South American tour ended in Buenos Aires under the guiding hand of Miguez Bonino. To all outward appearances it was a sophisticated city much like Paris, but one was soon aware that underneath it was a seething cauldron of discontent.

Nobody trusted the currency and we were advised not to change money at any of the banks; a much better deal could be obtained on the black market and, everybody, including the faculty at the theological college, used it openly. The degree of distrust and fear which prevailed was vividly illustrated for me when I inquired of the girl behind the counter at Braniff Airlines whether I could change any spare pesetas at the airport before catching my plane back to Europe. 'Oh no', she said, 'Nobody wants Argentinian pesetas. I don't know whether I'm going to get home alive tonight!' When we stepped off the aircraft on to English soil at Gatwick we felt that we were putting our feet on firm ground once more, whatever problems were facing our own country at the time. But the whole journey had been an unforgettable experience; we had seen something of a fascinating part of the world and had come to understand a little better the conditions under which so many of our fellow men and women lived.

Nevertheless, an unexpected problem awaited my return to Selly Oak. During the spring term a confrontation had arisen in Fircroft between the students and the Principal, and by the time I arrived back this involved the governors of the college as well as the tutors, and all four parties had got themselves into entrenched positions;

the students had voted to exclude the Principal from all teaching responsibilities; the tutors were also at loggerheads with him and the governors felt that, unless they supported him things would get completely out of control. There was nothing I could do unless invited to intervene; for Fircroft, like all the other colleges, was completely independent under its own governing body, and my writ did not run as far as its internal management was concerned.

By the beginning of the summer term things began to go from bad to worse, and at last in desperation the tutors, with the agreement of Christopher Cadbury, the chairman of the governors, asked whether I would approach Sir Robert Birley to see whether he and I could suggest any solution to the problem.

Sir Robert agreed to come at once and it was arranged that we should meet the tutors and the representatives of the students separately in my office during the evening and then see the governors on the following morning.

Sir Robert arrived in the late afternoon and we had two long meetings with the tutors and the students listening to their respective sides of the story. It was ten o'clock before we got back to my house, only to find that Marjory had received a telephone call from the chairman of the governors to say that they would not be able to see us the following day because they had to meet the staff and students to resolve the problem. This seemed inexplicable. Sir Robert had come all the way from Somerset to put his time and immense experience at the disposal of Fircroft and, after we had seen the tutors and students, we felt we had much to say to the governors before they should meet them. So I phoned Christopher Cadbury to protest against the arrangement we had made being cancelled, but he was adamant; his fellow governors could not see us; matters had reached a crisis and they must handle it themselves.

The next day was an extraordinary one. The governors met the students and staff and told them they would have to close the college. Naturally Sir Robert and I were accused of bad faith; there had been no point in our meeting with staff and students if a decision had already been taken to close the college; in the prevailing atmosphere of suspicion we were accused of having played a charade though we had been completely in the dark about the governors' intentions. Neither tutors nor students could be expected to believe that in the highly charged atmosphere.

It was a lovely summer's day and Sir Robert stayed until the evening in case the governors might wish to consult him; but they did not, and he returned to Somerton without a word of bitterness or resentment at the way in which he had been treated. He was looked after all day by Marjory in the garden, and she wrote an account of it with a sensitive appreciation of Sir Robert in a monograph published by a number of his friends after his death.

The situation at Fircroft had by then got out of hand. Protests to members of parliament and trades unions had blown the whole affair out of all proportion, and the students had resolved to take over the college and organize a sit-in. I offered to see whether I could suggest some way out of the impasse and Sir Robert agreed to come back to Selly Oak and meet the governors with me.

The meeting was held in a hotel in down-town Birmingham and the suggestion we made was to give the Principal a term's leave of absence and put Dr Ian Fraser, the Dean of Mission, in temporary charge. We believed that he had the confidence of both staff and students, and that this was the only way of rescuing an otherwise impossible situation. However, it was known that he was sympathetic to both students and staff and had been critical of the way in which the governors had handled the problem. This was too much for them. They had boxed themselves into a position from which they felt they could not retreat, and so they confirmed their intention to close the college and submit the whole dispute to a commission of inquiry set up by the Department of Education and Science.

The saga which followed was bizarre in the extreme. The commission of inquiry met for a week under the chairmanship of a leading QC and produced a devastating report which severely criticized all four parties to the dispute. In spite of this, the governors sought to find another way of reopening the college and appealed to the TUC to take over its management with a new board of governors on which they should have the majority of seats. This seemed to be agreed and a prominent member of the TUC General Council was nominated as chairman. But insufficient care had been taken to see if this would meet the requirements of the Charity Commissioners. It turned out not to do so; the terms of the Fircroft trust would not allow the TUC to take responsibility for what was an educational charity. This set the TUC and the Charity Commission at odds over the right of trade unions to engage in educational activity and the future of Fircroft seemed to be in danger of being lost sight of in the ensuing controversy.

At any rate the college governors and trustees had come to the end of the road and this seemed to be the moment to take a completely new initiative. The Chief Education Officer of the City of Birmingham, the Head of the Extra-Mural Department of the University, the Chairman of the West Midlands branch of the Workers Educational Association and I formed a consortium of four to explore a new way forward for Fircroft as a residential college of further education for mature students. To do this we had to be given a completely free hand and there really was no other option for Christopher Cadbury and his fellow governors.

Theirs had been a painful experience and this was particularly true of Christopher Cadbury himself. Fircroft was housed in his old home where he had grown up as a boy and he loved every inch of the ground; his father had founded the college and he had given much of his energy and time to its development. It had been a cruel blow to find himself vilified and his dream shattered. I hoped that we would be able to rescue what had been achieved from the wreckage and restore something of which he could be proud.

We had excellent co-operation from the Charity Commissioners and the Department of Education and Science. The former helped us to draw up a new instrument of government which satisfied the terms of the original trust and gave us freedom under independent auspices to develop the college in a way that would secure public recognition and funding. But it was the government officials who made the reopening possible; for without public funding there was no way in which we could have gone forward and there was every chance that we would not secure it. Only the persistent backing of the Assistant Secretary persuaded the Minister not to abandon Fircroft altogether after what had happened. When we secured confirmation that the finance was guaranteed for an initial period of five years, we were able to negotiate a lease of the building and grounds for the next twenty-five years and invite representatives of organizations named in the instrument of government to form the board of management. The next step was to find a new Principal and staff.

My three colleagues pressed me to be the chairman of the new board of governors at least for the first three years until we should have got the college established. This presented some difficulty as I was about to retire from the Presidency of the colleges and did not want to stay around, breathing down the neck of my successor. However, I was persuaded that I could keep quite clear of the rest of the campus and concentrate entirely on Fircroft for which, it was felt, I had a background shared by nobody else and the confidence of all those directly concerned. So I agreed, and actually served for the maximum term of six years as chairman. Looking back, I think this worked reasonably well and without embarrassment to my successor or becoming involved in the affairs of the rest of the colleges.

So my life at Selly Oak was coming to an end and Marjory and I had to begin to think about the future. Where this would be and what we should do we did not know. I could hardly have expected it would turn out to be so challenging and rewarding.

Chapter Thirteen

THE OPPORTUNITIES OF RETIREMENT

Grow old along with me!
The best is yet to be,
The last of life, for which the first was made:
Our times are in His hand
Who saith, 'A whole I planned,
Youth shows but half; trust God: see all,
nor be afraid!'

THESE LINES from Robert Browning's *Rabbi ben Ezra* express better than anything else I know my conviction about growing older. I have believed this from the days of my youth and therefore would deny that I have a vested interest in quoting the words now that I am over eighty years old. Speaking to high school students, I used to tell them that it was the cruelest thing for anyone to persuade them that their teens were the happiest years in their lives or that the honeymoon was the peak of a marriage after which the relationship was bound to go downhill. If this were true, the young would almost have 'had it' and the future would hold little prospect for them. The Chinese know better in venerating age, and I am told that it is considered to be a compliment to tell anyone how old they are looking!

Therefore, I had always looked forward to retirement as an opportunity to do things I had never been free to do before, and so life began again at sixty-six. The years that followed were to prove more varied and interesting than I could possibly have foreseen. Indeed, although the Presidency of the Selly Oak Colleges was the most fascinating and fulfilling job I could have had, I would be hard put to it to make comparisons as far as satisfaction is concerned with the blessings of retirement and old age.

But first I had to persuade others that the time had come to hand over the reins to somebody else. The suggestion was made that I should stay on as President for another two years, but I felt that this would only delay the search for a successor and there was everything to be said for leaving before people wanted you to go. Besides, I had to face a new challenge which could not easily be met if I remained at Selly Oak.

Our William Paton Fellow in 1978 was a Central American Jesuit priest, Xavier Gorostiaga, who was also an economist with special interest in the Panama Canal. It was our practice to ask the William Paton and Dorothy Cadbury Fellows to present a report at the end of their stay summarizing their experience and making any suggestions they cared to put forward. Father Gorostiaga expressed his surprise that there was no research institute in Britain concerned with Christianity and Society, and recommended that this should be explored. It so happened that a week or so later Harry Morton, then Secretary of the British Council of Churches, brought his senior staff to Selly Oak for a day to see what plans the colleges had for the next five years, and they showed special interest in Father Gorostiaga's suggestion. But the problem was how this was to be taken any further. The upshot was that I was asked by the executive committee of the BCC to chair a working party to consider the kind of instrument that would be required to put the idea into effect, and it seemed that unless I was prepared to pursue the matter myself nobody else would do so. That was to lead to the establishment of the Foundation for the Study of Christianity and Society which was to occupy much of my time and energy over the next ten years.

But more of this later. A quite different challenge was presented at the same time. A general election was looming and I was asked whether I would stand as a Liberal candidate for the Selly Oak constituency. I had been a life-long Liberal, but I had never had the opportunity to take an active part in politics. So this, with the prospect of becoming deeply involved in the bearing of Christianity on political, social and economic questions, made it clear to me that the time had come to retire from the Presidency of the colleges, and the date was fixed for the end of March 1979 just after my sixty-sixth birthday.

The general election was to be called less than two months later, and Marjory and I moved into a small house in Selly Oak to prepare for the campaign. Standing as a Liberal in that constituency was, of course, a forlorn hope and I never expected by any stretch of the imagination to get elected. For many years the seat had been held for the Conservatives by Harold Guerdon until he had lost it by a wafer-thin majority at the last election to Tom Litterick, someone so far to the left of the Labour party that they had almost lost sight of him on its extreme fringes. The Tories were determined to redress what they considered to have been an inexplicable mistake, and Selly Oak was one of Margaret Thatcher's main targets. If their candidate, Anthony Beaumont-Dark, had not won the seat, there would have been no hope of a Conservative victory throughout the country.

I was quickly to discover the efficiency of the Tory machine. The constituency was one of the largest in Birmingham and was divided into three wards – Selly Oak, King's Norton and Moseley. In the third of these alone I was told that the Conservatives had 400 people working for them on the ground during the campaign. I had four! And in the middle of the afternoon on polling day I ran into the Conservative agent who asked me whether I would like to know the result of the election; he was able to predict it almost to a hundred or so votes. That was the extent to which his organization had tied up the whole constituency.

We were, of course, hopelessly squeezed. With the narrow margin between the Conservative and Labour candidates many people voted negatively to keep one or other of the main candidates out, and I was told by more than one sympathizer that they would have voted for me but could not bring themselves to do so for fear of letting one of the others win. All the same we collected over 5000 votes, the largest number for the Liberals in any of the Birmingham constituencies, and it was great fun. Charles and Daphne Crooks came down from Dalbeattie for three weeks to act as my agents and did a heroic job. Marjory and a friend climbed up lamp posts to put up posters and one of my former colleagues at Westhill toured the constituency with me in a loud-speaker van. We had at least raised the Liberal flag in Selly Oak and had caused some excitement. I was to make another political sally two or three years later by standing for the Liberals in Dalbeattie for the Dumfries and Galloway Regional Council. This time my opponent was the sitting Independent and, in spite of incurring the natural suspicion of being a Sassenach, I managed to secure a substantial proportion of the votes.

That was the extent of my actual political involvement, though I was to be engaged in thinking and writing on the subject in subsequent years. However, when the campaign for the general election was over, we packed up our belongings and settled down to an entirely new life in Dalbeattie. Neither Marjory nor I had ever lived in the country and, although her parents had originally come from Scotland, we had never contemplated making our home across the border. But we had fallen in love with Crinan Cottage and we found ourselves welcomed into a small and friendly community. Mention has already been made of Charles and Daphne Crooks, but we were also taken under the wing of the nearby farmer, Stanley Edmunds, and his wife Jenny who took pity on these English townsfolk who could not be expected to adjust to country ways without help and support. This led to a firm friendship and many were the occasions when Stanley would come to deliver a load of logs in his tractor or pull down a tree or rescue us when the well which provided our water ran dry. Marjory, too, found the Roman Catholic church in Dalbeattie a lively community where she was made to feel at home. She quickly made a number of friends and had leisure to pursue her research on Dryden. So we began to settle down and the thought of moving anywhere else gradually receded.

The train service from Dumfries to Birmingham and London was a good one, and I was able to make frequent journeys south in the interests of Fircroft, the Foundation and other ecumenical commitments. Fircroft took a good deal of time. First of all we had to find a Principal. We were fortunate in securing Brian Wicker of the extra-mural department of the University of Birmingham where he had been lecturing in English literature. He was a man of many parts, well known for his writing on peace studies, philosophy and theology in which subject, as a prominent Roman Catholic layman, he had established quite a reputation. Brian fitted admirably into the ethos of Selly Oak and he had just the broad sympathies and fertile imagination to develop a new pattern of adult education at Fircroft. The next steps were to appoint the tutorial staff and draw up the curriculum for the first intake of students.

We were also fortunate in having inherited Pam Davies as our bursar. She had kept the wolf from the door during the long period of the dispute and its aftermath by raising the standard of catering and hospitality to the point where Fircroft had become an attractive venue for conferences and short courses. This provided a solid administrative base on which to build, and I managed to persuade a leading business man, David Livingstone, the chairman of Albright and Wilson, to become the treasurer.

At first all was not plain sailing by any means. The former tutors were on the warpath, campaigning to become reinstated and threatening to have Fircroft blacklisted in the Trades Union movement unless we gave in to their pressure. Of course, there was no way in which we could have yielded or considered their reinstatement; an entirely new start with new personnel was necessary if there was to be any chance of securing public support. We weathered the storm of the preparatory year and after that sailed into smoother waters.

There was, however, one bizarre and baffling occurrence which took place some time later. The former senior tutor, Harry Newton, suffered from a bad heart condition and died not long after the college had become re-established. One morning a national newspaper carried the extraordinary story that someone had disclosed that Harry Newton was in the employ of MI5 and had been used to infiltrate the Campaign for Nuclear Disarmament. Nobody who had known Harry well at Selly Oak believed this could possibly have been true. Harry was in many ways a lovable figure, but wholly unstable and unpredictable; it was inconceivable that he should have been employed in any secret intelligence mission while he was at Fircroft and, if so, it would have cast a serious reflection on the competence of MI5. Harry was much too busy making trouble for those with responsibilities at Selly Oak. All the same, strange things took place in those days and what was happening in the intelligence world defied all rational analysis. But nobody has ever given any credible explanation of how the story that appeared in the press came to see the light of day.

At first I had agreed to serve as chairman of the Fircroft governors for an initial term of three years, but my colleagues on the board persuaded me to continue for a second term not only to preserve continuity, but to handle negotiations for the renewal of funding as the end of the five-year guarantee approached. This proved to be more difficult and the outcome more uncertain than when we had first negotiated the reopening of the college. But I had in David Livingstone, the treasurer, a redoubtable ally and a strong board of governors who could point to the obvious success of what had been achieved. But the personnel at the Department of

Education and Science had changed, and government policy was based on a rigorous drive to get value for money. To defend the expensive cost of a residential college, however successful it might be and however imaginative its programme, was no easy task in the prevailing climate.

Arrangements were eventually made for the senior civil servant responsible to the Minister for all major decisions to come to Fircroft and assess the situation at first hand. A date was fixed for a certain evening and David Livingstone and I arranged to be there. I had to come from a conference in Derbyshire and David, whose business commitments took him all over the world, had rearranged his diary to make himself available. When I arrived at Fircroft in the late afternoon, the Principal told me that he had just received a telephone call from the civil servant to say that he could not meet us that evening because he had to have dinner with someone, but he would be coming the next morning instead. To this the Principal's protests had been unavailing. Such lack of consideration was beyond excuse. After all, as a civil servant. whatever his rank, he was paid to do the job, whereas David and I were giving our services at some considerable inconvenience. However, David very generously agreed to come back again the following morning and I arranged to stay overnight at the college.

When the civil servant arrived the next morning he showed not the slightest sign of being aware of the inconvenience or offence he had caused and his arrogance tried our patience to the limit, but we were in his hands; he would decide whether Fircroft would have any future or whether all we had worked to achieve would come to nothing. In the end we won a reprieve, and I was able to hand over the reins to my successor as chairman with the assurance that in the short term at any rate the college's future was guaranteed. But the experience impressed upon me how helpless the average citizen is in the face of officialdom when the power of the purse strings is in the hands of anyone with an exaggerated sense of his own importance.

While Fircroft took up a good deal of my time in the first five years of my retirement to Scotland, my major preoccupation was with the tentative steps to forge an instrument for undertaking fresh thought about the contribution Christians might make to the shaping of British society. The initial working party had reached the conclusion that what was required was not a research institute with a paid staff and an expensive headquarters for which there was no sign of funding being available. The favoured alternative was a loose network of concerned people from various walks of public life who could be encouraged to meet together, share their common experience and stimulate one another to bring influence to bear on the decision-makers and, by writing or broadcasting, address themselves to the problems facing our society.

To pilot this project and to give it standing and authority it was decided to invite a small group of representative people in public life to form an advisory council and Lord Blake, the Provost of the Queen's College, Oxford agreed to act as chairman. I began by setting four hares running to see what would be the most productive method of proceeding. From the outset I was clear that some or all of them might have a limited life or simply lead to dead ends; if they did we should learn something from them.

Living in Galloway, Scotland seemed the place to start. Through the co-operation of Professor Duncan Forrester of New College, Edinburgh and under his leadership a group of academics from the four old Scottish universities of Edinburgh, Glasgow, Aberdeen and St Andrew's met a number of times to discuss papers they had written about the problems facing the country north of the border. This proved to be both stimulating and useful, though it became clear that these discussions had a limited life and would not be a constituent part of any ongoing role for the Foundation. However, after Professor Forrester became Principal of New College he initiated a programme of consultation and research covering the same field and at the time of writing this is beginning to bear fruit.

One thing, however, was a personal bonus from the experience of this group. I was enabled to understand more sympathetically how very different the problems of Scotland appear to be when living there from the way they are perceived south of the border. When I first came back from Canada I went to see the Secretary of the Overseas Board of the Church of Scotland to explore the possibility of their candidates sharing in the mission programme at Selly Oak. I remember my surprise when he said, 'But Edinburgh is such a *long* way from Birmingham!' For a Canadian the distance was negligible: little more than a normal car ride to visit a friend. But I was to learn that distance is not necessarily measured in miles; the feel can be much more significant. In spite of the fact that students came to Selly Oak from every other part of the world, they never came from Scotland where training was retained in Edinburgh, although our first two Deans of Mission were ministers of the Church of Scotland!

Living in Galloway simply reinforced this perception of emotional distance. English people recognize that the Scots have different judicial and educational systems, though they may find this a bit puzzling. But they are misled by the assimilation of expatriate Scots into the English way of life into supposing that north of the border it feels the same as living in the south. It does not. I was constantly reminded of the feel of radical distance when crossing from Canada to the United States and vice versa. The growth and influence of the Scottish National Party is frequently misunderstood as a peculiar and passing aberration on the part of politically frustrated people; it is much more than that; it is the reflection of a sense of distinctiveness which is far more widespread than the SNP and is deeply felt by many of those who have no desire for complete political independence. That is why the Scots view their national Church as bound up more closely with their destiny than the English regard the Church of England.

That is not altogether a digression; for it is a reminder that the problems of political devolution are deep-rooted and complex; what is applicable in one place may not be so elsewhere. This ties in with the second hare I set running. I was conscious of the danger of the Foundation being too generalized and of being criticized for setting up nothing more than a talk-shop. Arising out of my political interests it seemed to me that there was a need for Christians to look at the future of local government, particularly in the light of the way local congregations might play a part in developing a sense of community and how it should be ordered. I, therefore, invited a small group of people with direct experience of local government either as councillors or officials to meet and explore the whole question. We were fortunate in persuading Professor Michael Fogarty to chair the group which comprised three chief executives of local authorities as well as a number of others with wide experience of different aspects of the subject.

We met at regular intervals over two years at the Policy Studies Institute in London at the end of which Professor Fogarty produced a valuable report which, while identifying a jungle, argued that it was fertile and open to Christian influence. The report had much to say of importance about the future of local government and about the contribution that Christians could make to it, but it did not lend itself to publication as it stood. The SCM press therefore commissioned me to write a book based upon it which was published in 1986 under the title *Government by the People?* and followed a more general one issued two years earlier entitled *Politics and the Christian Vision*. Unfortunately, the one on local government appeared with a picture on the front cover of Ken Livingstone against a red background which put a lot of people off even looking at it, though the book actually had nothing whatsoever to do with him. At the time it was assumed by the publisher that Ken Livingstone was the symbol of local government which turned out to be an unfortunate mistake. But the book and the report behind it still stand and seem to me even more relevant eight years later than when they were first written. The future of local government has become increasingly problematic in the light of the centralizing tendencies that have been seen to be increasingly apparent as time has passed.

The third project was based at Westminster College, Oxford, and brought together a group of scientists to look at the bearing of the subject on the problems facing contemporary society. This had the shortest life of any of the four hares I had started running. It came to focus on the need to pay attention to scientific education in the schools where a narrow and value-free scientism was seen to be all too pervasive. Although the group did not continue to meet for very long, it had at least uncovered a problem that would not go away and had to be addressed by those concerned with a Christian approach to education.

The fourth project has had the longest life and has developed into an on-going programme of study. It began with a group in Birmingham chaired by Bishop Lesslie Newbigin concentrating on the question of what the Bible has to say about the problems of contemporary society. The group, which included several laymen, met for about two years and came up with a number of questions addressed to biblical scholars, the essence of which was the bearing of their work on the political, social and economic problems confronting us today.

This led to Bishop Newbigin and me going to see Professor George Caird, the leading New Testament scholar at Oxford, to put before him the difficulty the group had found in relating academic biblical studies to the problems with which they were trying to wrestle. Caird listened sympathetically to what we had to say, and his response was that we were asking for a new direction in biblical scholarship; the only way to make any progress was to bring together a group of young scholars to face the issue. We asked him whether he would be prepared to chair a colloquium and invite a selected number to join it. He generously agreed to do so and to draw up a list of those whom he would invite. Unhappily he died from a heart attack not many days later.

We were, however, fortunate in securing the consent of Professor Robin Barbour of Pitlochry to take over his mantle and issue the invitations. There was an immediate and enthusiastic response and the first colloquium was held at Fircroft College, attended by about fifteen Old and New Testament scholars from Glasgow, Sheffield, Oxford, Cambridge, Durham, Nottingham and Southampton who expressed their appreciation at being challenged to face questions that were not really being addressed in their learned societies. A programme of study was agreed and the group has now met annually for a residential weekend and for smaller day consultations in between, producing papers and working towards future publications. These are beginning to appear, the first of which was a short book edited by Professor James Dunn of the University of Durham, entitled *The Kingdom of God and North East England* (SCM, 1986), based upon meetings between biblical specialists and those engaged in practical projects in that region. It is to be followed up by a book I have written entitled *The Kingdom of God: Fact or Fiction* to be published early in 1995. But the most important result thus far has been the recent issue of a symposium by members of the group, edited by Professor Barbour, entitled *The Kingdom of God and Human Society* (T. & T. Clark, 1993). The range of studies has been extended each year and is perhaps the most promising outcome of the Foundation.

The result of this preliminary exploration was the decision to establish a forum of up to twenty people with a wide experience of different phases of public life who would meet for residential weekends and hopefully initiate pieces of work which would lead either individual members or small groups to publish their findings. Subjects like work and leisure, and the effectiveness or otherwise of the different Churches' pronouncements on public questions have occupied the attention of the forum. The model has been 'The Moot', the group brought into being by J. H. Oldham during and after the Second World War, consisting of people like Karl Mannheim, T. S. Eliot and Sir Walter Moberley, the value of which was that they influenced one another though the results were often intangible.

I and those associated with me, like Bishop Lesslie Newbigin and Bishop Robin Woods, have now handed over to younger people the responsibility for taking this kind of exploration further, but looking back on the limited achievements of the past ten years there are two reflections which underline the difficulty of what we have tried to do. The first is the problem of securing the necessary financial support for such an undertaking. The Foundation has operated on a shoe string provided by a few grants from trusts and with no assured means of continuing support. What we have done has depended very largely on the willingness of people to give their services, but that has its inevitable limits. The basic problem is that initiating fresh thinking does not command the confidence of those who have funds at their disposal and who are much more ready to contribute to what they see as practical projects which have tangible results. This applies to the Churches no less than to charitable trusts; they are preoccupied with financing their own ecclesiastical concerns, and serious research, to the importance of which lip service is given, has a very low priority in practice. The fear is that money set aside for thinking is wasted in talk, and that is hard to combat. But, as Bishop David Jenkins once said when we were discussing the problem, 'See what a mess we've got into by neglecting long-term thinking for short-term pragmatism!' Unless people can be persuaded that hard thinking is important and is the prerequisite for rational practice, those who engage in the sort of enterprise the Foundation has initiated will face a precarious future.

The second and unsolved problem is one of communication. It

became increasingly clear that, if the work we were undertaking was to bear fruit, ways would have to be found for making the results not only known, but intelligible and relevant, first of all to the man and woman in the pew, but also to the public at large. Publication of books at that level is becoming more and more difficult, and there do not appear to be forthcoming those who have the imagination to do for another generation what C. S. Lewis was so strikingly successful in doing during and after the last war. Reference has already been made to the frustration in failing to make any real impact by the work we had done on local government. That was no doubt largely due to my own limitations, but an imaginative leap was necessary of which none of us seemed capable. That is a problem we have to bequeath to others, though Lesslie Newbigin has done more than anyone else to point the way. All the same I do not regret the time and effort put into launching the Foundation. Perhaps this is one of the many flowers that should be encouraged to bloom and, if some of them wither and die, others must take their place. I leave unanswered the question whether over the coming years the Churches have to exercise their mission to our society in the public sphere by spawning a variety of fringe initiatives free from ecclesiastical constraints, or whether a more concerted effort has to be made to grapple with the problems that confront our society as we approach the dawn of a new millennium.

Chapter Fourteen

A SECOND RETIREMENT

THE FIRST FIVE YEARS of retirement at Crinan Cottage were very happy ones. Marjory and I were kept very busy; the surroundings were beautiful, the people friendly, and we both enjoyed good health. But we knew that it would not make sense to stay in Galloway much longer. We were getting older and the isolation of the cottage would become more and more difficult as time went by; frequent journeys to London were becoming more tedious and we were far away from our family. The crunch came when our daughter in the Midlands telephoned to find out whether we would be down south and able to baby-sit while she and her husband were away. The thought of 250 miles of motorway between us whenever a crisis arose was too much to contemplate and so we decided to make the break, reluctant as we were to leave a place which we had found so idyllic.

Where were we to live? The decision finally rested on a good centre of communications with convenient road and rail links, and we settled on Banbury, finding a house in the nearby village of Middleton Cheney. I was still fully occupied with the Foundation and the International Association for Mission Studies, but new and quite unexpected responsibilities were to fall to my lot, coinciding almost exactly with our move down south.

Since 1942 I had been a member of the Reform Club in London, which I had joined as a young man during the war as a place where I could get away from West Ham; it has one of the finest libraries anywhere and convenience of access meant that I could easily spend a day there without being disturbed. When in later years I have been asked who make up the membership of over 2000, my

The Reform Club

reply has been that it comprises a complete cross section of public life divided into three categories: those who use it to get away from other people, those who find it a convenient place for entertaining guests to lunch or dinner, and those who choose to make it a club and enter into its social life. During my time at West Ham I fell into the first category and simply used it as a place of escape. Then, when I went to Canada, I retained an overseas membership, finding it a suitable base in London whenever I needed to spend a night there. But until my retirement, in spite of having been a member for nearly forty years, I had taken no real part in the life of the club and knew very few of its members.

This was to change quite dramatically. In the early nineteen-eighties the club had run into financial difficulties with a substantial loss on the food services and an accumulating annual deficit which showed no signs of being reversed. At the annual general meeting there was a good deal of restiveness and I was brash enough to make a speech saying that the drift must be brought to an end. This met with a warm response and subsequently the trustees intervened to insist upon the appointment of a catering committee to which two members of the club with expertise on the provision of food services should be co-opted. They were charged with turning a deficit into a surplus which they proceeded to do within four months.

I suppose that my speech led to me being nominated for membership of the General Committee. At any rate I was elected and after the first year's apprenticeship found myself appointed to the chairmanship of the House and Fabric committee. This gave me responsibility for one of the finest buildings in London. It had been designed by Barry, the architect of the Houses of Parliament, following the founding of the club in 1836 by supporters of the Reform Bill of 1832. The building was Barry's masterpiece with a handsome staircase leading to the gallery above, cleverly designed with mirrors to cast reflections on the saloon below. The placing of the staircase enabled the centre of the ground floor to be free for the square saloon under an arching dome of glass. Owing to financial stringency little had been spent on the building for a number of years and so there was a considerable back-log of work to be done which was gradually put in hand. The club was approaching the sesquicentenary year of its foundation, and under the capable chairmanship of Geoffrey Drain, the former general secretary of NALGO, plans were made for the celebration. This included an exhibition of material from the archives covering much nineteenth-century political history when the club was the centre of Liberal party activity, and it was opened by the Duke of Gloucester.

The General Committee asked me to organize a service of thanksgiving in St James's Piccadilly at which Viscount Tonypandy, one of our honorary members, gave the address. This was arranged for a summer's evening in June 1986 and the body of the church was filled for the occasion. Four years earlier membership of the club had been opened to ladies and the sesquicentenary was marked by the election of Dame Mary Donaldson, the first woman Lord Mayor of London, and Dame Tiri Te Kanawa as honorary members.

In 1987 I was elected chairman of the club in succession to Geoffrey Drain and held this office for the next two and a half years. This occupied a great deal of my time and proved to be a fascinating experience of an entirely different kind to anything I had been involved in before. The period was notable for the election of the Duke of Gloucester and Dr Garret Fitzgerald as honorary members, each of whom addressed the club at dinners arranged in their honour. It was also notable for the participation of lady members in the General Committee; there were three of them out of the total complement of fifteen and each of them chaired one of the six sub-committees. Considering that by then ladies accounted for only about a tenth of the club membership, this was a high proportion and underlined the fact that the Reform Club had become fully liberated and had broken with the tradition of male exclusiveness which still dominates London clubland. That was finally confirmed by the election of one of them, Mrs Barbara Coulter, to the chair of the General Committee in 1992: an event which caused quite a stir in the national press. All but a bare handful of hardened traditionalists and male chauvinists are now agreed that the club has become a more gracious and attractive place for their presence. At all events it flourishes and I am grateful to have had some small part in it.

This second retirement was, therefore, a very full one; for besides the Reform Club there was writing to be done as well as my commitments to the Foundation and the International Association for Mission Studies. Nevertheless, a shadow fell over these years. Two months after we had moved from Scotland to Middleton Cheney I returned from a visit to London to find that Marjory had been to see the doctor with a suspected lump in her breast and this was diagnosed as cancer requiring an operation for its removal. For the next four years she waged a courageous battle against the spread of the disease, but it attacked her lungs and then her spine, and although the drugs retarded it, she gradually became weaker. The last phase leading to her death is such a wonderful story of medical care and her response to it that it should be told, not least because the National Health Service comes in for so much criticism. Marjory's story is of care far beyond anything anybody could have asked for or expected.

In November 1987 I had to go to Rome for an IAMS committee and I left Marjory with my brother and his wife in Leicestershire while I was away. On my return I was met by my brother on the doorstep to be told that Marjory had been taken ill that day with breathing difficulty and that an ambulance was on the way to take her to the Royal Infirmary in Leicester. I was just in time to go with her and to agree that a tracheotomy had to be performed to maintain an airway with an artificial tube. The operation was a success, but she returned home very frightened; it had proved to be the last straw and she did not know how to face the future.

When our excellent GP, Dr Large, came to see her, he said it was beyond him and he would have to call in a specialist. Within a quarter of an hour he was on the telephone to tell me that the specialist was on his way and would be meeting him at our house within the hour. The consultant turned out to be Dr Michael Orr who was then in charge of the whole psychiatric department of the Oxfordshire Health Authority. After coming into my study and listening to the GP's report, he went in to see Marjory and spent half an hour with her. On returning to the study he changed the medication, said he had found her very frightened, and would take on the case. Dr Orr came every other day for a fortnight, spending half an hour each time with Marjory, and on the alternate days he telephoned me to find out how the treatment was progressing. As a Roman Catholic he had established immediate rapport with Marjory and by the end of the fortnight he had made her angry with the tracheotomy, convinced her that her rebellion against it did not incur the anger of God and had brought her through to complete peace of mind and readiness to face the future whatever it might be.

Within a few days, however, she contracted a severe infection of the lung and kidneys and our GP said there was nothing else to do except to have her admitted to the Michael Sobel Unit, the hospice attached to the Churchill hospital at Oxford. The next five weeks were a triumph of the spirit over a rapidly weakening body. Marjory communicated her faith and courage to staff, patients and visitors alike. From her bed she sent messages to all her friends and to those she had known throughout her life; indeed, the joke was made that she would have been running up a considerable bill for the National Health Service if she had not been using the volunteers for dictating short letters!

But an unforgettable feature of these five weeks was the three visits of Dr Michael Orr. He had finished his treatment while Marjory was still at home, but he came to see her in the Sobel unit on three occasions, on the second of which he left a picture of the Virgin and Child for her to look at as long as she was there. Such imaginative kindness was far beyond anything anyone could have expected, and crowned what had been a remarkable combination of medical skill and theological insight. Ten days before she died the staff arranged a birthday celebration for my small grandson, wheeling Marjory's bed, decorated with balloons, into the day room. The end was not long delayed. As the sister in charge watched her life draw to a peaceful end, she turned to me and said, 'What a beautiful death'. Indeed it was, both beautiful and triumphant and, although grieved, I could not but be profoundly grateful.

The requiem mass was held in Banbury, and a large congregation assembled of those who had known and loved Marjory. They represented a wide ecumenical spectrum testifying to the catholicity of her life and interests: the Ecumenical Society of the Blessed Virgin Mary, the West Ham Central Mission, the Selly Oak Colleges, the Reform Club, and the local Roman Catholic and Baptist congregations. The first to receive communion was Dr Michael Orr, and among those who could not do so but came forward for a blessing were an Anglican bishop and our own GP. Marjory was buried in the churchyard of her parish at Aston-le-Walls.

After Marjory's death I had to begin life again at the age of seventy-five. That may be said to mark my third retirement. I was still involved with the Foundation and the International Association for Mission Studies and my chairmanship of the Reform Club had not yet come to an end, but all three commitments were due to be handed over to others within the next few months. So I thought this would be the time and opportunity to look up old friends and make plans for whatever the future might hold. That led me to invite Dorothy White to have lunch with me at the club.

She had been one of the young members of the staff at the West Ham Central Mission during the war, responsible for the evacuation of those who were bombed out of their homes during the blitz of the Luftwaffe on London's dockland. She had left in 1944 to take up a nursing career at the London hospital, and our paths had not crossed for forty-four years except for a chance encounter in 1959 when I was on my way to the University of Leeds in the interests of McMaster. As I was waiting for the train on the platform of King's Cross station I recognized someone I thought I knew, and it was Dorothy, also en route to Leeds. We travelled in the dining car and exchanged news. It turned out that she had risen through the ranks and had just been appointed Deputy Chief Nursing Officer at the Ministry of Health with responsibility for advising ministers on nursing policy. She was going to Leeds to confer with people in the health service there and we parted on the platform. I had occasionally heard of her and knew that she had had a distinguished career, recognized by the award of the OBE in 1967. She had retired in 1976 and I found that she was living in Eastbourne.

Our meeting for lunch in London led both of us to decide to share the rest of our lives together, though it was a brave thing for a professional woman to do after paddling her own canoe for so many years. We were married in February 1989 and I came to live in her flat overlooking the sea just below Beachy Head. In her retirement Dorothy had set up St Wilfrid's Hospice in Eastbourne and she was deeply involved with St Saviour and St Peter's, the main Anglo-Catholic church on the south coast, as well as in serving on the diocesan and deanery synods. Trained as a professional singer in her youth, she had given this up to work at West Ham where, in the absence of our regular organist on active service in the RAF, she had deputised for him, playing for the broadcast services during the war. In the choir of St Saviour's she had found that she was able to use her musical gifts, and this was obviously her spiritual home.

It, therefore, made sense for me to express my ecumenical convictions by participating in the life of St Saviour's, and I was warmly welcomed and encouraged to do so by the vicar, the late Canon Derek Allen. Subsequently I have been asked whether I have become an Anglican, to which my reply has been that I am an ordained Baptist minister and will remain so to the end of my days; for that is where my roots are. Denominational differences now seem to me to be of little importance and those who remain wedded to dogmatic and divisive formulae appear to me to be splitting theological hairs out of all proportion to the common confession of the Christian faith. I was privileged to be present as a representative of the British Council of Churches when the Pope visited Canterbury Cathedral. For me the most significant feature of that service was when the Pope, the Archbishop of Canterbury

With Dorothy on the Black Prince

and the Moderator of the Free Church Federal Council stood side by side on the chancel steps and declared together their common faith.

Divisions between the Churches remain and inter-communion is still contrary to the rules laid down by the Roman Catholic and Orthodox Churches. But things have changed dramatically over the last thirty years. When I returned from Canada in 1965 I was unable to receive communion in many Anglican churches. That is no longer the case; Anglicans and Free Church people for the most part share in one another's eucharists. The position *vis-à-vis* Roman Catholics today is not unlike that obtaining between the Church of England and the Free Churches in the nineteen-sixties; the rules forbid it, but they are frequently broken particularly on the mainland of Europe. It is difficult to see how they can be sustained for much longer; the experience of pilgrimage together in many localities will make separation at the Eucharist increasingly hard to defend. The rules are not likely to be changed in my lifetime, certainly not under the present pope, but the movement towards full inter-communion is inexorable, and behind it is the impulse of the Spirit.

Structural integration of the Churches is not a goal worth pursuing, save in terms of economizing wherever possible; the wastage of personnel, money and buildings is deplorable where they hinder co-operation and could be shared. But Christians will always differ in their forms of worship, theological emphasis and the means of organizing their common life. Variety is not only the spice of life, but also the essence of Christian freedom. For me denominational differences do not matter. Inter-communion is what is essential as well as the freedom to share in the faith, life and witness of my fellow-Christians who with me acknowledge Jesus as Lord.

As I look back on over eighty years I can say with the Psalmist, 'Goodness and mercy have followed me all the days of my life'.

The gracious and loving hand of God may be discerned in the blessings of my home and upbringing, in the road which led me from West Ham to Canada, to Selly Oak and then to a fruitful and happy retirement. Above all I thank God in every remembrance of Marjory and the undeserved bonus of these closing years with Dorothy. She has cared for me in my growing physical disability with wonderful devotion and I do not know how I would have managed without her.

As I look to the future, it is with faith and hope. The passage of time has increased my curiosity and loosened my dependence on dogmatic formulations of belief which are inevitably relative. Growing older has the benefit of confirming how little we know. But it can also bring us to the simplicity of that on which we ultimately depend. In the last resort faith for me means that life's mysteries are resolved in the redemption of the world by the life, death and resurrection of Jesus Christ on whom all my hopes for this world and the world to come are grounded. So in the closing years of my ecumenical pilgrimage I remember with gratitude and look forward with hope.

INDEX

INDEX